CIRC   {CASTL}   M6/649285
KEO 706 A315 0685 1986
C. 1
ONTARIO.
THE CHILD AND FAMILY SERVICES ACT

D0054177

DATE DUE

APR 1 9 1988 4/141	
(JAN 3 1 1989)	
MAR 8 1989	
MAR 0 9 1992	
MAR 1 6 1994	
APR 1 5 1995	

BRODART, INC.   Cat. No. 23-221

THE CHILD AND
FAMILY SERVICES ACT

THE CHILD AND FAMILY SERVICES ACT: A GUIDE TO PART III

DOUGLAS W. PHILLIPS
AND
DOUGLAS J. MANNING

Butterworths
Toronto and Vancouver

SELKIRK COLLEGE LIBRARY
CASTLEGAR, B. C.

The Child and Family Services Act: A Guide to Part III
ⓒ 1986 Butterworths, A division of Reed Inc.

All rights reserved. No part of this publication may be reproduced, stored in a retrieval system, or transmitted, in any form or by any means (photocopying, electronic, mechanical, recording, or otherwise), without the prior written permission of the copyright holder.

Printed and bound in Canada by John Deyell Company

The Butterworth Group of Companies

Canada:
Butterworths, Toronto and Vancouver
United Kingdom:
Butterworth & Co. (Publishers) Ltd., London and Edinburgh
Australia:
Butterworths Pty Ltd., Sydney, Melbourne, Brisbane, Adelaide and Perth
New Zealand:
Butterworths (New Zealand) Ltd., Wellington and Auckland
Singapore:
Butterworth & Co. (Asia) Pte. Ltd., Singapore
South Africa
Butterworth Publishers (SA) (Pty) Ltd., Durban and Pretoria
United States:
Butterworth Legal Publishers, Boston, Seattle, Austin and St. Paul
D & S Publishers, Clearwater

Canadian Cataloguing in Publication Data

Ontario.
   [Child and Family Services Act, 1984]
   The Child and Family Services Act: a guide to part III

Previously published as the Child Welfare Act
R.S.O. 1980, C 66.
Includes index.
ISBN 0-409-80524-6

1. Children - Legal status, laws, etc. - Ontario.
2. Parent and child (Law) - Ontario. 3. Ontario.
Child and Family Services Act, 1984. I. Ontario.
Child Welfare Act, 1980. II. Phillips, Douglas W.
III. Manning, Douglas J. IV. Title.

KE0706.A3150685 1986   344.713'0327   C86-093715-1

Sponsoring Editor: Paul Truster
Managing Editor: Linda Kee
Supervisory Editor: Marie Graham
Editor/Cover Design: Catherine Haskell
Production: Jim Shepherd
Typesetting: Computer Composition of Canada Inc.

FOREWORD

Those of us who have been active in the Family Law field, whether as practitioners, judges or other professionals have, in recent years, seen fundamental changes in both the procedural and substantive provisions contained in the legislation with which we work each day. The most recent of such statutes, *The Child and Family Services Act, 1984* is a complex and multi-faceted work which not only repeals *The Child Welfare Act* and other major pieces of legislation but, in some way, modifies an additional nineteen statutes.

In that changing environment which has often reflected major shifts in social concepts, it is critical to our performance that we have available to us comprehensive yet clear, concise and practical reference materials.

Messrs. Phillips and Manning have approached their subject, Part III of the Act relating to child protection in a manner which will be particularly helpful to those of us who will use as a starting point in understanding and applying this new legislation, *The Child Welfare Act* with which we are familiar.

Part III of the new Act is in some respects substantially different from Part II of its predecessor. In certain cases the differences are subtle at first glance but in time those subtleties may prove to have significance. The style of this text addresses those differences both obvious and subtle in a very pointed and understandable way.

Each section of the new Act is set out with reference made to the comparable section or sections of *The Child Welfare Act*. A commentary is included which emphasizes the points of similarity and the differences with the predecessor Act. The authors have not been timid in their treatment of the legislation in that potential difficulties in interpretation are addressed with suggested resolutions where appropriate. The case law which follows each section includes significant cases under *The Child Welfare Act* and which, in the initial period following the coming in to force of the new Act, will be critical to an understanding of its meaning.

It is not, I suspect, an easy task to produce a text which serves both readers who require a practical and more general understanding of legislation and, as well, those who have the need for a more detailed treatment. Messrs. Phillips and Manning have, I believe, achieved both objectives.

In short, this is a thorough and highly useful work. It will, I am certain, be viewed as a needed and practical contribution to the field of Family Law. It will be read profitably and provide to a broad range of professionals an ongoing and significant tool.

His Honour Judge Robert J. Abbey
Provincial Court (Family Division)
County of Essex

PREFACE

The purpose of this book is to serve as a practical reference source to Part III of the *Child and Family Services Act, 1984* S.O. 1984, c. 55 relating to child protection. The book is intended primarily for solicitors practising in the Provincial Court (Family Division), but it should serve as a useful guide to the legislation for professionals working at all levels in the field of child welfare.

The design is based, in the main, upon a section by section review of Part III dealing with the protection of the child. A beginning portion deals with the Declaration of Principles which is included at Section 1 of the Act; from there the analysis moves to Part III, where the protection sections begin, covering from Section 37 through Section 83.

The *Child and Family Services Act* is the direct successor to the *Child Welfare Act* R.S.O. 1980, c. 66, (hereafter referred to as the "old Act") among three other pieces of legislation designed to aid children (16 other pieces of legislation are modified). Most of the sections of the new Act derive directly from sections in the old Act, some with no change at all, many with minor modifications, and many with major change of wording and intent. Some of the sections of the new Act are brand new. Like many of the modifications of the existing sections, they most often reflect the changes in the direction and emphasis which make up a "new approach" to child and family law in Ontario.

Many solicitors who have worked for years with the *Child Welfare Act* will now find the climate different in very many respects. In the writing, we have therefore attached great significance to the *Child Welfare Act* as the derivative source of the current provisions on protection. Equivalent sections are identified throughout and attention is drawn to all major changes and most minor ones.

Each section of Part III of the *Child and Family Services Act* is of course, reprinted in full in the section-by-section analysis. Frequent references are made in the Act, and in our text, to sections which are in some part of the Act, other than Part III. (The new Act has twelve parts.)

Finally, the commentary and analysis which accompanies each section of the new Act, are followed in many cases by summaries of the important cases. Cases are for the most part, those decided under the *Child Welfare Act,* or its equivalent legislation in other provinces. The selection of these cases is designed to give the reader guidance as to the way the *Child and Family Services Act* counterparts are likely to be interpreted. The cases have been decided under other pieces of legislation and therefore are not binding upon the judges of our courts but merely persuasive.

ACKNOWLEDGMENTS

The authors wish to express their gratitude to William G. Phillips to whom they are deeply indebted for his tireless efforts towards this text. His comments and assistance in the organization, style and content of this work proved invaluable. Mr. Phillips' contributions of time and experience provided a depth to the work that the authors could not have otherwise accomplished.

The authors also wish to acknowledge the contribution and assistance provided to them by the Law Foundation of Ontario, and the partners of the law firm, Mousseau, De Luca, Hilbers, Dinham, Phillips, Porter and Favot.

TABLE OF CONTENTS

The Child and Family Services Act

Part III: Child Protection

Table of Contents

TABLE OF CASES

THE CHILD AND FAMILY SERVICES ACT

SECTION 1. DECLARATION OF PRINCIPLES

HER MAJESTY, by and with the advice and consent of the Legislative Assembly of the Province of Ontario, enacts as follows:

1.   The purposes of this Act are:
   (a)   as a paramount objective, to promote the best interests, protection and well-being of children;
   (b)   to recognize that while parents often need help in caring for their children, that help should give support to the autonomy and integrity of the family unit and, wherever possible, be provided on the basis of mutual consent;
   (c)   to recognize that the least restrictive or disruptive course of action that is available and is appropriate in a particular case to help a child or family should be followed;
   (d)   to recognize that children's services should be provided in a manner that:
      i. respects children's needs for continuity of care and for stable family relationships, and
      ii. takes into account physical and mental developmental differences among children.
   (e)   to recognize that, wherever possible, services to children and their families should be provided in a manner that respects cultural, religious and regional differences; and
   (f)   to recognize that Indian and native people should be entitled to provide, wherever possible, their own child and family services, and that all services to Indian and native children and families should be provided in a manner that recognizes their culture, heritage and traditions and the concept of the extended family.

COMMENTARY

This is a gathering together of the basic principles upon which the *Child and Family Services Act* is founded. Its inclusion in the legislation is new, though the principles themselves (with the exception of that at paragraph (f)), are not. Indeed, it could be argued that the statement of principles is in reality only a codification of the court practice and case law which have accumulated under previous enactments, particularly, the *Child Welfare Act.* Regardless, the inclusion of the Statement should prove a useful addition to the law. Not only does it give legislative authority to the principles themselves; as we shall see in the frequent references to it which follow, it also reveals the rationale behind many of the directions taken and the emphases given throughout the Act. In some instances, it may even be the essential ingredient in the interpretation.

The one clear departure in the Statement of Principles refers to the special case of Indian and native people at clause (f). The unique cultural and customary practices of these social groups are recognized and provided for throughout the Act. Part X, in fact, is devoted entirely to the service of the Indian and Native child. As do the other clauses, clause (f) of the Statement of Principles reflects the evolution of social thought and values in Ontario. The autonomy and integrity of the family, the desirability of stable family relationships, of help by mutual consent and with the least possible disruption: all these are the approach to child and family problems which by now has become fundamental in Ontario.

Missing from the Statement of Principles is any reference to the desirability of prevention of problems before they arise. Many may view this with misgiving, noting that neither the word nor the idea of prevention is included in the Statement. Indeed, no such reference is made before section 15(3)(c), and then only as a general "function" of a children's aid society. Thus the widespread yearning to see greater emphasis on prevention included in legislation, especially in social legislation, remains unfulfilled in this case.

Finally, the inclusion of a Statement of Principles seems much in keeping with the sweeping coverage of the new legislation, which offers in one package what were previously a number of hazily related laws pertaining to the problems of children. The list of the statutes that have been repealed or modified to make way for the *Child and Family Services Act,* is a long one, to which the Statement of Principles gives an element of cohesion, a needed common reference point. The collection of affected laws is found in Part XII of the Act.

PART III
CHILD PROTECTION

SECTION 37. DEFINITIONS

This section sets out the important definitions of words and phrases used throughout Part III.

It has four definition subsections: GENERAL (subsection (1)); PROTECTION (subsection (2)); BEST INTERESTS (subsection (3)) and INDIAN and NATIVE PERSON (subsection (4)).

I GENERAL

S. 37(1)(a): Definition of a Child

(a)   "Child" does not include a child as defined in paragraph 6 of subsection 3(1) who is actually or apparently sixteen years of age or older, unless the child is the subject of an order under this Part.

The definition of "child" in the *Child Welfare Act* was at s. 19(1)(a).

COMMENTARY

In the new Act a child is defined, for general application within the Act at s. 3(1)(6), as "a person under the age of eighteen years." Once a person reaches the age of 18 years, or marries, the court's jurisdiction under Part III ends (see s. 67(1)).

For the particular purposes of child protection, however, a distinction is introduced, which separates a child less than 16 from a child who is 16 but less than 18 years old.

Thus, for protection purposes, a "child" is:

(1)   any person who is less than 16 years of age;
(2)   any person who is 16 years but less than 18 years of age, *and* is the subject of an order made under Part III.

Despite the neatness of this test, the legislators foresaw the difficulty where a child's 16th birthday occurred between the commencement of a proceeding or apprehension and delivery to court. At s. 43(3) a further exception permits a court to deal with a child 16 or over where:

(1)   the child was apprehended; or
(2)   a proceeding under Part III was commenced;

while the child was 16 years. A proceeding is defined as commenced with the filing of an application.

The term "order" was not defined in the *Child Welfare Act* nor does the 1984 Act supply a definition. The meaning in Part III however, is probably abundantly clear from the context. The following are the *principal* orders provided for:

(1)   An order refusing to make an order (s. 3(1)21.);
(2)   An order directing legal representation for a child (s. 38(3));
(3)   An order to produce or apprehend a child (s. 40(3));
(4)   An order that a child remain in a place of open temporary detention (s. 42(2));
(5)   In cases of adjournment, a temporary order for care and custody (s. 47(2));
(6)   An order for assessment of a child or a parent or other person in charge of the child except a foster parent (s. 50);
(7)   A supervision, society-wardship or Crown-wardship or a combined society-wardship and supervision order (s. 53);
(8)   Where no court order is deemed necessary an order to return the child to the person previously in charge (s. 53(9));
(9)   An access order or any order thereafter varying or terminating such access (s. 54);
(10) A payment order where the court places a child in care of a society or a person other than the child's parent (s. 56);
(11) An order determining the rights that a parent shall retain to give or refuse a consent to medical treatment for a child (s. 58(1));
(12) A court-sanctioned medical consent by a society for a child who is a society ward (s. 58(3));
(13) An order for review of a previous order (s. 61).

Quere: does a warrant under s. 40(2) constitute an "order" for which the implications of s. 37(1)(a) would apply?

CASE LAW s. 37(1)(a)

Re United Counties of Stormont, Dundas and Glengarry and Metro. Toronto, [1964] 2 O.R. 224, 45 D.L.R. (2d) 16 (C.A.).
An unwed mother under the age of 16 years is a "child" within this provision.

Re M.R. (1983), 36 R.F.L. (2d) 400 (Ont. Prov. Ct.).
Where a child becomes 16 years of age after the commencement of an application but prior to a final disposition and is the subject of an order pending the adjournment, the court retains its jurisdiction.

S. 37(1)(b): Definition of Child Protection Worker

"child protection worker" means a Director, a local director or a person authorized by a Director or local director for the purposes of section 40 (commencing child protection proceedings).

The Child Welfare Act's equivalent section was far less extensive at subsection (f) of s. 1(1).

COMMENTARY:

In the new act the definition relates to the procedure for bringing a child to court to determine whether such child is in need of protection. Such procedure is covered in s. 40, which is in fact the only section in which the term "child protection worker" occurs.

Thus the following three categories of person have authority to bring a child to court:

(1) A Director (for definition see s. 3(1) para. 13.); for some of the powers see ss. 17, 37(1)(e), 71, 72, 73, 74, 197(1)1.
(2) The local director of a Children's Aid Society (for definition see s. 3(1), para. 17. and s. 16).
(3) A person in the employ of the Children's Aid Society, who has authority from a Director or a local director to bring a child before the court. Such person is usually a Children's Aid Society worker.

S. 37(1)(c): Definition of Extended Family

(c) "Extended Family", when used in reference to a child, means the persons to whom the child is related by blood, marriage or adoption.

There was no equivalent section in the *Child Welfare Act.*

COMMENTARY:

This new provision will have its widest impact in considerations under s. 53(4) in which the court, before making an order for society or Crown wardship, is to consider the possibility of placing the child with a member of the extended family under the terms of a supervision order made under paragraph 1 of s. 53(1).

Considerations of the "extended family" also come to play a significant role in cases of Indian or native children (for some examples see ss. 53(5) and 57(2)(d)).

Introduction of "extended family" considerations bring into implementation the declared principles of the Act, as set out in s. 1(b), (c), (e), (f).

Ontario is evolving into a multicultural society with correspondingly diversified traditions, values and attitudes. The courts are now to consider the impact of these factors on a child's development and the possible consequences of disrupting the continued exposure to these factors when a child is removed from familiar surroundings.

It is interesting to observe that the "extended family" is not expressly referred to within the definition of "best interests", but may come into play in paragraphs 3., 5. and 13. of s. 37(3).

The term "family" is not defined within the Act, except within Part VIII dealing with *Confidentiality of and Access to Records*, where "family" is set out at s. 162(a). Further, the term "relative" is defined only in s. 130(1)(c) of Part VII concerning adoption.

The reference to extended family placement as an alternative to society or Crown wardship, within s. 53(4) of the new Act, in effect parallels the option for an order of placement with an "other person" under supervision, found in s. 30(1)1. of the *Child Welfare Act*.

S. 37(1)(d): Definition of Parent

(d)   "Parent" when used in reference to a child, means each of:
  (i)   the child's mother,
  (ii) an individual described in one of paragraphs 1 to 6 of subsection 8(1) of the *Children's Law Reform Act*, unless it is proved on a balance of probabilities that he is not the child's natural father,
  (iii) the individual having lawful custody of the child,
  (iv) an individual who, during the twelve months before intervention under this Part, has demonstrated a settled intention to treat the child as a child or his or her family, or has acknowledged parentage of the child and provided for the child's support,
  (v)   an individual who, under a written agreement or a court order, is required to provide for the child, has custody of the child or has a right of access to the child, and
  (vi) an individual who has acknowledged parentage of the child in writing under section 12 of the *Children's Law Reform Act*,
       but does not include a foster parent.

Its predecessor was s. 19(1)(e) of the *Child Welfare Act*.

COMMENTARY:

The term "parent" occurs frequently throughout the new law. Thus, it is an extremely important definition as well as one of the more complex.

First, the principal changes introduced in the 1984 legislation should be noted. In the 1984 definition of "parent" a guardian of a child appointed at law is no longer included. Moreover, it is possible for the Crown or a society to fall within the definition of "parent." However, a foster parent remains excluded from the definition.

Secondly, the definition of "parent" in s. 37(1)(d) should be viewed concomitantly with the provision of s. 3(2), which stipulates that,

> **s. 3(2) In this Act, a reference to a child's parent shall be deemed to be a reference to:**
> **(a)   both parents, where both have custody of the child;**
> **(b)   one parent, where that parent has lawful custody of the child or the other parent is unavailable or unable to act as the context requires; or**
> **(c)   another individual, where that individual has lawful custody of the child,**
> **except where this Act provides otherwise.**

The forerunner of this provision was s. 92 of the *Child Welfare Act.*

Third, s. 37(1)(d)(ii), quoted above, refers to s. 8 of the *Children's Law Reform Act* R.S.O. 1980, c. 68 which lists the circumstances giving rise to a presumption that a male person is the father of a child. Such circumstances are as follows:

1.   The person is married to the mother of the child at the time of the birth of the child.
2.   The person was married to the mother of the child by a marriage that was terminated by death or judgment of nullity within 300 days before the birth of the child or by divorce where the decree *nisi* was granted within 300 days before the birth of the child.
3.   The person marries the mother of the child after the birth of the child and acknowledges that he is the natural father.
4.   The person was cohabiting with the mother of the child in a relationship of some permanence at the time of the birth of the child or the child is born within 300 days after they ceased to cohabit.
5.   The person and the mother of the child have filed a statutory declaration under subsection 6(8) of the *Vital Statistics Act* or a request under subsection 6(5) of that Act, or either under a similar provision under the corresponding Act in another jurisdiction in Canada.

6.   The person has been found or recognized in his lifetime by a court of competent jurisdiction in Canada to be the father of the child.

CASE LAW s. 37(1)(d)

Re C.A.S. Metro. Toronto and C. (1979), 25 O.R. (2d) 234 (Prov. Ct.). The definition of "parent" in s. 19(1)(e) is not exhaustive and could include persons not referred to in the provision and therefore is entitled to notice.

R.C.C.A.S. Essex and Warren (1983), 44 O.R. (2d) 283, 37 R.F.L. (2d) 322 (Ont. Co. Ct.).
The s. 19(1)(e) definition of "parent" is exhaustive; thus where a person does not fall within the categories enumerated, he or she will not be a "parent" as defined. This case can be distinguished from *Re C.A.S. Metro. Toronto and C* based on the amendment to the definition.

Barlow v. Barlow (1978), 8 R.F.L. (2d) 6 (Ont. Prov. Ct.).
On an application under the *Family Law Reform Act* for support of the applicant mother's child of a prior relationship from a respondent husband who was not the father, the court examined the meaning and intent within the definition of "parent" of demonstrating a settled intention to treat as a child of his or her family. "The court found on the evidence that the respondent was the father, given that the child was known by the respondent's surname (though no formal birth registration change was ever made), took the child to school and supported the child. In addition, relative to a child born of the marriage the court found the respondent's treatment of both to be without "apparent difference." The court determined in addition that the Act did not require the continued expression of such intention after separation or to trial of the support application in order to have the respondent remain within the definition for support purposes. The court found that such a proposition would be "rendered virtually ineffective by the many fathers who are alienated shortly before applications to court." Furthermore, the respondent was unable to utilize a separation agreement wherein the parties had identified the one child born of them as the child for support purposes (and thereby excluded the other child, the subject of the application) as a defense or as demonstrative of a revocation of "settled intention". The intention once demonstrated and found to have so existed by the court caused the respondent to fall within the definition of "parent".

C.A.S. Ottawa-Carleton v. D.J.L. and L.J.T.L. (1980), 15 R.F.L. (2d) 102 (Ont. Prov. Ct.).
On an application for Crown wardship by way of a status review

under s. 32(1) of a supervision order the court stated "that the term parent includes not only natural parents but other persons who have assumed or may assume a parental role . . . It is now recognized that this significant relationship may exist or may develop between a child and other than natural parents". In short that there should be no presumption in favour of natural parents.

Macdonald and Macdonald (1979), 24 O.R. (2d) 84, 97 D.L.R. (3d) 763 (Co. Ct.).
The court interpreted the meaning of "demonstrated settled intention" found in the *Family Law Reform Act* definition of "parent" to mean more than the provision of support by a respondent to a child. Provision of financial support, while a factor, was not conclusive. The court considered it a requirement on the evidence to examine whether a respondent was "fulfilling other parental duties and responsibilities . . ." before such a finding would be made. The onus of proof for the imposition of such status upon a person rested with the applicant.

S. 37(1)(e): Definition of Place of Safety

(e)   "Place of Safety" means a foster home, a hospital, and a place or one of a class of places designated as such by a Director under subsection 17(2) of Part I (Flexible Services), but does not include:
   (i)   a place of secure custody as defined in Part IV (Young Offenders), or
   (ii) a place of secure temporary detention as defined in Part IV.

Its predecessor was s. 19(1)(f) and (g) of the *Child Welfare Act.*

COMMENTARY:

The new definition is open-ended insofar as under s. 17(2) referred to above, "a Director may designate a place as a place of safety . . . for the purposes of Part III (Child Protection)". Nevertheless, in addition to the two places named as acceptable – a foster home and a hospital – others are named as unacceptable. A child subject to Children's Aid Society intervention cannot be placed in "secure custody", or in a place of "secure temporary detention." In the instance of "secure custody", reference is made in the Act to s. 24(1) of the *Young Offenders Act* S.C. 1980-81-82-83, c. 110. What precisely a "place of secure temporary detention" means will have to await promulgation of regulations under s. 200(1)(a), (b).

Excluding such restrictions, a child who is the subject of Part III process will be placed in:

(1)   a foster home;
(2)   a group home;
(3)   a hospital, medical or other treatment facility;
(4)   a place designated by a Director under s. 17(2).

II PROTECTION

S. 37(2): Circumstances for Protection

Subsection (2) defines the need for protection by listing the circumstances under which that need exists. These circumstances include:

(a)   physical harm
(b)   substantial risk of (a)
(c)   sexual molestation or exploitation
(d)   substantial risk of (c)
(e)   need for medical treatment
(f)   emotional harm
(g)   substantial risk of (f)
(h)   a mental, emotional or developmental condition
(i)   abandonment
(j)   under 12: has killed, seriously injured a person; or damaged property
(k)   under 12: has repeatedly injured another; or caused loss or damage to property
(l)   parent unable to care for child.

These will be covered in order.

> **S. 37(2)(a) the child has suffered physical harm, inflicted by the person having charge of the child or caused by that person's failure to care and provide for or supervise and protect the child adequately;**
>
> **(b) there is a substantial risk that the child will suffer physical harm inflicted or caused as described in clause (a);**

The predecessor provisions in the *Child Welfare Act* were a combination of a number of the clauses of s. 19(1)(b).

COMMENTARY:

Subsection (2)(a) is clear, but the risk element in clause (b) requires interpretation. It is the first of three which introduces the "risk" element. It would appear that the element of risk must be real and material and must expose the child to the probability of harm. Risk must apparently be caused by the person having charge of the child if the reference to clause (a) is to be meaningful. However, given the construction of clause (a) it may also be taken to include other persons, whose contact with a child is as a direct result of the custodial person's failure to act responsibly.

S. 37(2)(c): Sexual Molestation

(c) **The child has been sexually molested or sexually exploited, by the person having charge of the child or by any other person where the person having charge of the child knows or should know of the possibility of sexual molestation or sexual exploitation and fails to protect the child;**

This is a new provision for which there is no direct *Child Welfare Act* s. 19(1)(b) equivalent. However, there may be some degree of compatibility to subclauses (iv), (v) and (xi) of s. 19(1)(b) of that Act.

COMMENTARY:

The contrasting language between new and old probably reflects the increasing of the public awareness of the problem. In addition, it is a recognition of the legislators' preparedness to use explicit language in referring to "sexual offences", though the Act still lacks a specific definition or catalogue of criteria setting out the meaning of "sexually molested" or "sexually exploited."

A careful reading of s. 37(2)(c) reveals that there are two requirements to be met before a child will be found in need of protection within this provision.

1. The child must have been sexually molested or exploited, and
2. This must have been done by,
   (a) the person having charge of the child, or
   (b) any other person where,
      (i) the person having charge knows or should know of the possibility of molestation or exploitation, and
      (ii) the person having charge of the child fails to protect the child against such possibility.

There are no guidelines for determining whether in any given situation there is a "possibility" of sexual molestation or exploitation. Further, the words "knows or should know" ought to be read as imposing the civil standard of the reasonable person. That is, would a reasonable person know, or should a reasonable person know, of the possibility of sexual molestation or exploitation.

11

S. 37(2)(d): Risk of Sexual Molestation

(d)   There is a substantial risk that the child will be sexually molested or sexually exploited as described in clause (c);

This is a new clause for which there was no equivalent in the *Child Welfare Act.*

COMMENTARY:

As in s. 37(2)(b), this clause gives an extra dimension to the preceding one by adding the risk element. There would seem to be some possibility of ambiguity in the application of "risk" in clause (d) to clause (c) – not with reference to the person having charge of the child but with reference to that person's knowing of the "possibility" of molestation or exploitation by another person. At the least, it would appear that the element of risk must be real and material ("substantial"), such that the child would *likely* be sexually molested or exploited. The risk may emanate from the person having charge of the child or from any person in contact with the child.

s. 37(2)(e): Need of Medical Treatment

(e)   The child requires medical treatment to cure, prevent or alleviate physical harm or suffering and the child's parent or the person having charge of the child does not provide, or refuses, or is unavailable or unable to consent to, the treatment.

The *Child Welfare Act* predecessor can be found in s. 19(1)(b)(ix).

COMMENTARY:

The striking difference in the 1984 provisions is the apparent narrowing of the application potential. The earlier Act referred to "medical, surgical or other recognized remedial care or treatment", while its successor refers only to "medical treatment." The purpose of such treatment has likewise narrowed – from being "necessary to the child's health and well-being" to being required "to cure, prevent or alleviate physical harm or suffering." On the other hand, the former criterion "recommended by a legally qualified medical practitioner" is not included, suggesting a wider permissible interpretation of the word "requires". In sum, the new formulation is more direct, and simpler: it refers only to the case where a requirement exists and nothing is being done about it. Presumably the court will decide between any opposing views as to whether such a requirement does in fact exist.

S. 37(2)(f): Emotional Harm

(f) **The child has suffered emotional harm, demonstrated by severe**
   (i) anxiety
   (ii) depression
   (iii) withdrawal, or
   (iv) self-destructive or aggressive behaviour,
   and the child's parent or the person having charge of the child does not provide, or refuses or is unavailable or unable to consent to, services or treatment to remedy or alleviate the harm.

The equivalent *Child Welfare Act* provision was s. 19(1)(b)(x).

COMMENTARY:

The 1984 provision concentrates on the fact of emotional harm and on the question whether treatment is being provided or will be consented to by the person having charge of the child. Unlike its predecessor, the 1984 law does not concern itself with the cause of the emotional harm, or with attributing the responsibility for such harm to any person. What is required is:

(a) evidence that is demonstrative of any of the four behavioural categories listed, and
(b) evidence that the person in charge is not providing the needed services or treatment, or is unable or refuses to consent to these.

S. 37(2)(g): Risk of Emotional Harm

(g) **There is a substantial risk that the child will suffer emotional harm of the kind described in clause (f), and the child's parent or the person having charge of the child does not provide, or refuses or is unavailable or unable to consent to, services or treatment to prevent the harm.**

This is a new clause for which there was no *Child Welfare Act* equivalent.

COMMENTARY:

The element of risk to the child is required to be "substantial", which suggests that it be material and real, not merely transitory.

The source of the substantial risk is not required to be specified or demonstrated when (g) is read in conjunction with (f). However, for all practical purposes, evidence would have to be presented illustrating the probable cause of possible anxiety, depression, withdrawal or self-destruction or aggressive behaviour of the child. This follows from the fact that, under clause (f), four categories of demonstrable behaviour are provided as criteria against which to demonstrate that emotional harm has in fact already been suffered. Under clause (g), the risk that emotional harm *might* occur would normally have to be assessed in the absence of any such criteria.

The source of such evidence would normally have to be medical, psychiatric, psychological or other mental health expertise. This same observation applies to clauses (h), (i), (j) and (k). The role of the parent becomes critical. (See commentary at s. 37(2)(j)).

S. 37(2)(h): Condition Emotional:

(h)   The child suffers from a mental, emotional or developmental condition that, if not remedied, could seriously impair the child's development and the child's parent or the person having charge of the child does not provide, or refuses or is unavailable or unable to consent to, treatment to remedy or alleviate the condition.

There is no direct equivalent in the *Child Welfare Act.*

COMMENTARY:

Clause (h) recognizes a distinction between

(1)   emotional harm as in clause (f) above which has been suffered at some time in the past (and presumably is still being suffered), and is now manifesting itself in the child's behaviour; and
(2)   a condition which as in clause (h), presently exists and is of a continuing nature.

The condition must be such that, if not remedied, it "could seriously impair the child's development".

While clause (f) includes behavioural criteria from which some previous emotional harm is to be inferred, clause (h) includes no criteria from which to infer the existence of such "condition." It is necessary then, under clause (h), to show

(a)   that such a condition exists, and
(b)   that the parent or the person in charge of the child is unable or refuses to consent to the services or treatment needed.

The wording here is the same as in clause (f) except for the words "harm" and "condition".

It is suggested that the distinction between these terms may give rise to difficult questions of causation. That is to say, does the former refer to the life experience of the child and the latter to a genetic or congenital state? One might expect the situation anticipated in clause (h) to be found only in exceptional circumstances. Where such cases do exist, there seems little doubt that specialized evidence of a professional nature would be needed to assist the court.

S. 37(2)(i): Child Abandoned

> (i) **The child has been abandoned, the child's parent has died or is unavailable to exercise his or her custodial rights over the child and has not made adequate provision for the child's care and custody, or the child is in a residential placement and the parent refuses or is unable or unwilling to resume the child's care and custody.**

The *Child Welfare Act* equivalent was s. 19(1)(b)(ii) and (iii).

COMMENTARY:

The criteria are now:

(1)   abandonment or,
(2)   the unavailability of the parent to exercise custodial rights where no adequate alternative provision has been made; or
(3)   the parent's refusal or inability to resume care of a child who has been in a residential placement.

There are points of similarity with the previous Act. The first criterion is essentially the same as in the *Child Welfare Act*; it would seem that "abandoned" and "deserted" can be taken to describe similar conditions. At whose hands the abandonment must be occasioned would presumably be the person having charge of the child.

The second condition is similar between the two Acts insofar as "unavailable . . . and has not made adequate provision", means substantially the same as "cannot for any reason care properly for the child."

The third circumstance within s. 37(2)(i) is new. It gives rise to a protection finding where the parent refuses to, or is unwilling to, resume the care of a child upon return from residential care. Presumably this reflects the inclusion of Part II, *Voluntary Access to Services* in the new Act, providing extensive remedies in the form of voluntary placement of a child. If a parent places a child voluntarily but does not accept the child's return, then such conduct may place the child "in need of protection."

S. 37(2)(j): Child Under 12 Has Killed or Seriously Injured a Person or Damaged Property

> (j)   **the child is less than twelve years old and has killed or seriously injured another person or caused serious damage to**

15

another person's property, services or treatment are necessary to prevent a recurrence and the child's parent or the person having charge of the child does not provide, or refuses or is unavailable or unable to consent to, those services or treatment.

This is a new provision for which there is no direct *Child Welfare Act* s. 19(1)(b) equivalent.

COMMENTARY:

The clause directs intervention in a child's life where the *Young Offenders Act* R.S.C. 1980-81-82-83, c. 110 has no jurisdiction, *i.e.* for a child under the age of 12 years.

The ingredients require:

(a)   that the child be under 12 years of age;
(b)   that the child has killed or seriously injured some person or seriously damaged property;
(c)   that a service or treatment is required in order to avoid recurrence; and
(d)   that the parent does not, refuses, is unavailable or is unable to consent to provide such service or treatment.

The age ingredient is straightforward. The matter of another's death is equally objective. However, in the case of injury, the use of "seriously" as applied to "injury" would connote something grave but less than gross. The same test might be applied to the "damage" to property.

Furthermore, the treatment or service to be used to deal with the child must be identifiable; and it must be demonstrated that such treatment or service will affect the child's conduct, and will have some probability of ensuring non-recurrence. The role of the parent or person having charge of the child must be put to the test as a condition before protection will be determined.

S. 37(2)(k): Child Under 12 Years Repeatedly Caused Injury or Damage

(k)   **The child is less than twelve years old and has on more than one occasion injured another person or caused loss or damage to another person's property, with the encouragement of the person having charge of the child or because of that person's failure or inability to supervise the child adequately.**

As with s. 37(2)(j) there is no *Child Welfare Act* equivalent.

COMMENTARY:

This clause is likewise intended to deal with children outside the ambit of the *Young Offenders Act* S.C. 1980-81-82-83, c. 110.

The ingredients to be made out are:
(a) the child's age;
(b) repeated injury to another person or repeated damage to a person's property;
(c) that (b) has been done with the encouragement of the child's custodian or because of lack of supervision by such person.

Clause (k) clearly intends to apply a less rigid standard than (j). The use of the terms "seriously injured" and "serious damage" in (j) has been reduced to "injured" and "loss or damage" in (k). Moreover, a single occurrence is not sufficient; it must be a repeated occurrence.

In a similar vein, there is no question of services or treatment to prevent recurrence in clause (k). It would seem that if the child has done the acts described, the child is presumed to be in need of protection. The question of the child's intent is not considered. A case could be envisioned where a child might be declared in need of protection whose conduct was simply accidental.

The clause is complicated by the inclusion of references to the conduct of the person in whose care the child is placed. Determining whether the child's action is a result of such person's encouragement or lack of supervision, will require that a careful investigation of such person be made. Can it be presumed that a custodial person is under all circumstances responsible for a child under 12? The answer in each case, will reflect the child's age (under 12), maturity, level of intellectual development, emotional makeup, and the degree of connection between the supervision and the injury about which the complaint is made. Is the parent guilty of a lack of "adequate" supervision, for example, where an 11-year-old child damages a window en route home from school?

The refusal of the parent or person in charge of the child to consent to treatment services is not an appropriate consideration in clause (k), as it was in clause (j). This is presumably the case given that it is a repeated act which had not been given remedial attention previously by the custodian. Thus, there is little incentive to provide the custodian with the opportunity to respond on a subsequent occurrence.

S. 37(2)(l): Parent Unable to Care for Child

(1) the child's parent is unable to care for the child and the child is brought before the court with the parent's consent and,

where the child is twelve years of age or older, with the child's consent to be dealt with under this Part.

The *Child Welfare Act* section most akin to clause (1) was s. 19(1)(b)(i).

COMMENTARY:

Two ingredients have been added:

(1)   that the parent is unable to care for the child; and
(2)   a 12-year-old child must give consent to being dealt with under Part III.

Point (2) is of extreme importance to the section. The absence of the child's consent will deprive a society and parents who are in agreement, from use of the section, and require a search for another criterion of protection.

The new clause, however, has to be seen in the light of s. 51, which recognizes the seriousness of any situation which could result in the removal of a child from a parent's care and custody, solely on the ground that the parent is unable to care for the child, and even where consent of the parent (and the child, if over 12) has been given. Section 51, as will be seen below, adds safeguards in the form of questions the court must ask, and points on which it must be satisfied, before any such removal order could be made by the court. A further safeguard exists in the blanket requirement in s. 53(1), that any order made by the court in protection cases must be made "in the child's best interests."

Having regard for the section comparisons at Table I between the *Child Welfare Act* and the *Child and Family Services Act* it appears that only s. 19(1)(b)(viii) has been completely dropped. Habitual absence from school is no longer in and of itself sufficient to constitute protection. Nor does such absence constitute an "offence" under the *Young Offenders Act* S.C. 1980-81-82-83, c. 110. (see s. 2(1)).

CASE LAW s. 37(2)

D. v. C.A.S. of Kent County (1980), 18 R.F.L. (2d) 223 (Ont. Co. Ct.). The onus of demonstrating protection is not that of the balance of probabilities *per se;* nor is there a test akin to the onus in criminal matters. No magic formula need be devised other than the heavy onus on the director of the Children's Aid Society to satisfy the court the allegations necessary to intervene are met and clearly met without reference or deference to the second issue (best interests) after a (protection) finding is made.

Re C.A.S. Kenora and J.L. (1981), 134 D.L.R. (3d) 249 (Ont. Prov. Ct.)

The *Child Welfare Act* does not preclude a finding that a child "en ventre sa mère" is in fact a child for the purpose of the Act. The conduct of a parent during pregnancy may be evidence demonstrating the need of protection.

Re M.T. (1983), 36 R.F.L. (2d) 386 (Ont. Prov. Ct.).
Where a child threatens suicide upon termination of a sexual relationship with an adult, he may be found to be in need of protection.

Re S. (1979), 10 R.F.L. (2d) 341 (Ont. Prov. Ct.).
The word "abuse" is not found in s. 1(b) (definition of "best interests of the child"), nor in s. 19(1)(b) (definition of a "child in need of protection"). Nevertheless, the wording in subsections (1) and (2) of s. 47 relates to the wording found in parts of both s. 1(b) and s. 19(1)(b). Furthermore, s. 47(3) directs the court to proceed as though the child had been brought before it as a child apparently in need of protection.

Re D. (1983), 22 Alta. L.R. 228, 30 R.F.L. (2d) 277 (Prov. Ct.).
A child was apprehended and, on the basis of medical advice, given a blood transfusion over the parent's religious objections and without their consent.
    The court found that the child was in need of protection and adopted the leading cases inclusive of *Forsyth v. C.A.S. of Kingston and County of Frontenac*, [1963] 1 O.R. 49, 35 D.L.R. (2d) 690 (H.C.J.), *Pentland v. Pentland and Rombough* (1978), 20 O.R. (2d) 27, 5 R.F.L. (2d) 65 (S.C.), and *Re Wintersgill* (1981), 15 Sask. R. 435, 131 D.L.R. (3d) 184 (Unified Fam. Ct.). The court also ruled that an objection based on the freedom of conscience and religion provisions in s. 2(a) of the *Canadian Charter of Rights and Freedoms* did not apply and stated: "as between the state's right to safeguard the health and welfare of children and the rights of parents to freely practice their religion, the former must prevail. If a responsible adult refuses to accept a blood transfusion for himself or herself on religious grounds, the state should not and will not intervene, but when medical treatment, that is, a blood transfusion is withheld from the offspring of the adult, the state must and has valid legislation to intervene."

III BEST INTERESTS

S. 37(3): Best Interests: Introduction

(3)   **Where a person is directed in this Part to make an order or determination in the best interests of a child, the person shall take into consideration those of the following circumstances of the case that he or she considers relevant.**

COMMENTARY:

The opening of this subsection directs the court to the ingredients of "the best interests of a child." These are the criteria which the court or other person is obliged to take into consideration in any section of the law where the "best interest" test is directed. These sections deal primarily with the making of orders or determinations, and they include the following:

(1) 53:   a court making an order for supervision by the society, or for society wardship or Crown wardship, or a combination of society wardship or subsequent supervision,

(2) 54:   a court making, varying or terminating an order respecting access to the child,

(3) 55:   a court making an order for access when a child has been removed from the person who had charge,

(4) 57(6):   a Director or local director removing a child from a foster home or other residential placement,

(5) 58:   a court making an order for medical treatment for a society ward where a parent refuses or is unavailable for consent,

(6) 60(10): a court deciding in whose care and custody a child remains until an application for status review is disposed of,

(7) 61(1):   a court considering an application for review, and in 61(3)(h) considering the least restrictive alternative to such review,

(8) 62(2):   a Director making the required annual review of Crown wards,

(9) 65(4):   a District Court, pending final disposition of an appeal, making a temporary order for the child's custody,

(10) 73(1): by a Director as to supervision or placement transfer of a child,

(11) 76:   the court making an order to restrain the access or contact of any person to the child,

(12) 77:   the Official Guardian instituting proceedings on a child's behalf to recover damages or compensation for abuse suffered by the child.

Throughout Part III, reference is made to the child's "interests". See ss. 38(2), (3) and 41(4)(a) for examples. Those references are not defined in the sense that "best interests" are, and are not, therefore, governed by s. 37(3). On the other hand, s. 37(3) defines over a broad 12-point range what constitutes "the best interest of a child".

S. 37(3): 1. Child's needs.

1.   The child's physical, mental and emotional needs, and the appropriate care or treatment to meet those needs.

The equivalent *Child Welfare Act* predecessor can be found at s. 1(1)(b)(i). The new language appears to say the same thing, and more clearly.

S. 37(3): 2. Child's Level of Development.

2.   The child's physical, mental and emotional level of development.

The equivalent *Child Welfare Act* clause can be found at s. 1(1)(b)(iii).

COMMENTARY:

Substitution of "level of development" for the former "stages of development" gives a here-and-now connotation which might have left some ambiguity in the earlier Act. This minor modification might also reflect a change in the legislators' attitude towards differing theories of child development.

S. 37(3): 3. Child's Cultural Background.

3.   The child's cultural background.

COMMENTARY:

This paragraph is new. The key word is "cultural". *The Shorter Oxford English Dictionary* defines in part the noun "culture" from which this adjective traces its meaning, as "the training and refinement of mind, tastes and manners; the condition of being thus trained and refined." Evidence of upbringing and conditioning appears then to have a legitimate place in the overall determination of "best interests."

Undoubtedly, as well, the inclusion of "cultural background" as a criterion of "best interests", is a recognition that a variety of new cultural additions have been, and are being made to Ontario's society, and in these, the family is the most important repository of the traditions, refinements of mind, tastes, and manners that make up each culture.

S. 37(3): 4. Child's Religious Faith

4.   The religious faith, if any, in which the child is being raised.

This paragraph is new. There is no equivalent provision in the *Child Welfare Act* which would make the religious faith in which the child is raised a required consideration. There is, however, a broad category referred to in the *Child Welfare Act* s. 1(1)(b)(iv) which requires the court to consider "the effect upon the child of any disruption of the child's sense of continuity."

COMMENTARY:

The new specific inclusion of religious faith appears to recognize the importance of this "sense of continuity", and so the difference in intent is probably not great. The religious beliefs and practices that a child has been taught can be a very integral part of that child's total make-up, probably more so than in most adults; and any needless disruption in that sphere could have highly unsettling effects on the child. Moreover, the religious mosaic has extended well beyond the traditional division between groups of Roman Catholics and Protestants, which simply opens a wider possibility of disruption to children if religion is not taken into account.

S. 37(3): 5. Child's Relationship to Parent and Family

5.   **The importance for the child's development of a positive relationship with a parent and a secure place as a member of a family.**

The equivalent under the *Child Welfare Act* was s. 1(b)(vii). While the wording of this provision is different from that which appears in the *Child Welfare Act*, it is suggested that there is no real distinction to be made.

S. 37(3): 6. Child's Blood or Adoption Relationships

6.   **The child's relationships by blood or through an adoption order.**

COMMENTARY:

There is no paragraph within the *Child Welfare Act* that deals with the influence of blood relationships or the existence of adoption orders. The inclusion of the new paragraph is in keeping with the objectives of the Act as set out in s. 1, namely promotion of the integrity of the family, and the insulation of the family unit from intrusive state agencies.

It is noteworthy that these criteria appear within the "best interest" test for custody under the *Children's Law Reform Act* S.O. 1982, c. 20, at s. 24(2)(g).

S. 37(3): 7. Need for Continuity

7.   The importance of continuity in the child's care and the possible effect on the child of disruption of that continuity.

The equivalent provision of the *Child Welfare Act* was s. 1(b)(iv).

COMMENTARY:

While the clauses of the two Acts are substantially similar, the requirement under the new law, to recognize the importance of continuity of care in the child's life, is new. Even though that is not expressly stated in the *Child Welfare Act* such a consideration had been routinely made under that Act and as such there will be little change with the new legislation.

S. 37(3): 8. Society's Plan for Child's Care.

8.   The merits of a plan for the child's care proposed by a society, including a proposal that the child be placed for adoption or adopted, compared with the merits of the child remaining with or returning to a parent.

The equivalent provision of the *Child Welfare Act* was s. 1(1)(b)(v).

COMMENTARY:

The wording of the new pararaph is essentially the same as the old, but for the obligation that a society specifically address the possibility of adoption where that possibility exists. The task of comparing the advantages of return to a parent (or not) remains intact.

S. 37(3): 9. Child's Wishes.

9.   The child's views and wishes, if they can be reasonably ascertained.

The equivalent provision of the *Child Welfare Act* was s. 1(1)(b)(vi).

COMMENTARY:

The deletion of "preferences" from the old Act and the insertion of "wishes" results in a better reflection of what the court and counsel are often in search of in the court process. Thus, the new paragraph is more in line with practice and caselaw.

Reference to the ability to ascertain the child's views and wishes has been retained from the old Act. This is a reflection of the reality that obtaining children's "views and wishes" will differ from child to child, depending upon a variety of conditions, *e.g.* age, level of intellect and maturity, range of life experience, and so on. Otherwise no significant change exists.

S. 37(3): 10. Effects of Delay.

10.   The effects on the child of delay in the disposition of the case.

The equivalent section under the *Child Welfare Act* was s. 1(1)(b)(vii).

COMMENTARY:

The minor modification in the 1984 legislation seems merely to reflect the legislators' attempt to avoid a perceived redundancy within the use of the term "final disposition." It will be interesting to observe how the court system reacts to the thrust of this paragraph along with ss. 47(1) and 48, the intent of which seems clearly designed to protect the child against loss in the limbo of litigation.

S. 37(3): 11. Risk of Removal.

11.   The risk that the child may suffer harm through being re-moved from, kept away from, returned to or allowed to remain in the care of a parent.

The equivalent section under the *Child Welfare Act* was s. 1(1)(b)(viii).

COMMENTARY:

The ambit of this paragraph is wider than that of its predecessor. The court is to consider not only the effect of the child's returning to or remaining with his or her parents, but also the possible effects of removal of the child from his or her parents. This reflects the declared principle of s. 1(d) which gives emphasis to the child's sense of possibly negative ramifications of removal of the child from a parent, even in spite of the overall unsatisfactory condition of life in which the child may be found.

S. 37(3): 12. Degree of Risk

12.   The degree of risk, if any, that justified the finding that the child is in need of protection.

COMMENTARY:

This provision is new. At first glance it may seem that the court is being asked to "second guess" its finding of protection in that this paragraph requires consideration of the "degree of risk" that gave rise to the protection finding.

In practice, this paragraph will most likely be restricted in its application to cases involving defined events or occurrences, as opposed to ongoing conditions. For example, what is the likelihood of recurrence of an undesirable type of corporal punishment? Will the event be repeated? Such questions would not be relevant to a neglect, or nutritional deprivation circumstance that has existed for a considerable period of time.

Also, this factor may come into play on a status review. The court would, appropriately, ask and answer the questions posed above. However, some questions remain unanswered. On a status review, for example, to what extent must a court review the original protection finding to determine the degree of risk? Is there the possibility that on a status review, a court will find itself enmeshed in a review of evidence that constituted the protection finding at first instance? The caselaw appears to suggest quite clearly that on a status review the matter of "protection" is not to be re-litigated. (See commentary at s. 60).

S. 37(3): 13. Other

13.   **Any other relevant circumstance.**

COMMENTARY:

This paragraph is new. It becomes the "catch-all." The scope and ambit of the subsection will have to await judicial determination.

CASE LAW: S. 37(3):

Re F.M. (1979), 11 R.F.L. (2d) 120, at 129 (Ont. Prov. Ct.).
"The definition of 'best interests' of the child and its application to ss. 30 and 32 does not, in my opinion, constitute a change in the substantive law but rather is more correctly characterized as procedural in nature and is meant to function to enable the court to arrive at a just determination of the proceedings. In the absence of legislative direction the common law rules of construction apply and accordingly I am bound to give effect to the words of the Act without regard to the wishes of the litigants."

C.A.S. Ottawa-Carleton v. D.J.L. and L.J.T.L. (1980), 15 R.F.L. (2d) 102, at 110 (Ont. Prov. Ct.).
The best interests criteria leave unchanged the necessity of assigning substantial weight to the claims of the natural parents, but no extra

 SELKIRK COLLEGE LIBRARY
CASTLEGAR, B. C.

weight is to be assigned to the claims of the natural parents given that other persons may develop relations of some significance with the child.

R.N.M. v. Nutter (1984), 40 R.F.L. (2d) 360 (Ont. C.A.).
Where a trial judge determines that a child is in need of protection, and in the best interests of the child, that the parents be denied access; then to place a child with an aunt whose ability to deny access to the parents is questioned, constitutes a misapplication of the best interests test.

IV DEFINITIONS: INDIAN OR NATIVE CHILDREN

S. 37(4): Indian or Native Children

> (4) Where a person is directed in this Part to make an order or determination in the best interests of a child and the child is an Indian or native person, the person shall take into consideration the importance, in recognition of the uniqueness of Indian and native culture, heritage and traditions, of preserving the child's cultural identity.

There was no comparable subsection in the *Child Welfare Act*.

COMMENTARY:

The thread continues throughout the legislation, giving recognition to the importance of cultural and traditional ties, as in s. 37(4) above. The present clause confers special recognition in the case of such ties arising from a child's status as an Indian or native person. It reaffirms the status accorded to services to Indian and native children and families as already established in the Declaration of Principles in s. 1(f).

SECTION 38. LEGAL REPRESENTATION

This section's purpose is to establish the mechanics by which a child is entitled to legal representation in connection with a proceeding under Part III of the Act.

> S. 38(1) A child may have legal representation at any stage in a proceeding under this part.
> (2) Where a child does not have legal representation in a proceeding under this Part, the court,
>   (a) shall, as soon as practicable after the commencement of the proceeding; and
>   (b) may, at any later stage in the proceeding,
>   determine whether legal representation is desirable to protect the child's interests.

(3) Where the court determines that legal representation is desirable to protect a child's interests, the court shall direct that legal representation be provided for the child.

(4) Where,

(a) the court is of the opinion that there is a difference of views between the child and a parent or a society, and the society proposes that the child be removed from a person's care or be made a society or Crown ward under paragraph 2 or 3 of subsection 53(1);

(b) the child is in the society's care and,

(i) no parent appears before the court; or

(ii) it is alleged that the child is in need of protection within the meaning of clause 37(2)(a), (c), (f) or (h); or

(c) the child is not permitted to be present at the hearing, legal representation shall be deemed to be desirable to protect the child's interests, unless the court is satisfied, taking into account the child's views and wishes if they can be reasonably ascertained, that the child's interests are otherwise adequately protected.

(5) Where a child's parent is less than eighteen years of age, the Official Guardian shall represent the parent in a proceeding under this Part unless the court orders otherwise.

The equivalent section of the *Child Welfare Act* was s. 20; the equivalent of s. 38(5) was s. 19(4).

COMMENTARY:

The section first establishes the child's right to legal representation at any stage in any proceeding under Part III. Such representation may be appointed at any point in the proceeding. If the child does not have legal representation, the court is directed to determine whether such representation would be "desirable." Such a determination must be made near the outset of the proceeding; and it "may" be made, subject to the court's discretion, at any later stage.

Section 38(2) seems to say:

(i) wherever a child has no counsel, the court must make a determination whether counsel is "desirable", as soon as practicable in the proceeding;

(ii) even if the court decides under (i) that counsel is not desirable, it can take up the question again at any later stage of the proceeding, at which point it can find it "desirable."

Thus the court remains, as it was under s. 20(2) of the *Child Welfare Act,* the arbiter as to the desirability of legal representation, restricted only by the need to protect the child's interest.

The governing criterion in the determination is that of desirability. In a case where representation for the child is determined to be desirable (having regard for the child's interest), the court is obliged to go beyond inquiry and to appoint counsel. Presumably, in making a determination of desirability, the court may take any relevant matter into account. However, three situations are described in s. 38(4), in any of which legal representation must be deemed desirable and counsel for the child must be provided.

A close similarity exists between the old and the new in this respect. This can be seen in a comparison of s. 20(3) of the *Child Welfare Act*, and s. 38(4) of the new law, shown above. Somewhat condensed, the provision in the 1984 law is that legal representation must be provided if:

(a)   a difference of views exists (in the opinion of the court) between the child and a parent or the society, and the society is proposing a wardship;

(b)(i) the child is in the society's care and no parent appears in court;
    (ii) the child is in the society's care and the application for protection is based on s. 37(2)(a), (c), (f), or (h);

s. 2 (a) physical harm to child;
    (c) child sexually molested or exploited;
    (f) child has suffered emotional harm;
    (h) child suffers from an emotional condition.

(These last four clauses cover substantially what were the *abuse provisions of* s. 47(1) of the *Child Welfare Act*.)

(c)   The child is not permitted to be present at the hearing.

Subsection (4) seems conclusive. However, two points should be noted. First, though the criteria are established, a court nevertheless remains at liberty to disregard the need for representation given the proviso at the concluding portion of subsection (4) *viz:* "unless the court is satisfied, taking into account the child's views and wishes . . ., that the child's interests are otherwise adequately protected."

Secondly, where the child is neither in care nor excluded from the hearing, the criteria seem to continue to preclude representation (as a requirement) where an application seeks supervision with a person other than the one in whose care the child was. The criteria though, are subordinate to the test which overrides, found in s. 38(2), "the child's interests".

It appears, therefore, that automatic representation is by no means established by statute. The right to representation is not enshrined; it is the subject of a number of provisos.

The Official Guardian has the responsibility to act for the parent under 18 years of age. This is in contrast to the *Child Welfare Act* where the court might appoint, "any other person" to be the guardian.

CASE LAW S. 38

Re C., (1980), 14 R.F.L. (2d) 21 (Ont. Prov. Ct.).
The court engaged in a discussion as to the role of counsel for children and made these points:

(1)   Where a child is "intellectually, socially and developmentally mature enough to express clear and consistent instructions" counsel should act upon and advocate those to the court;
(2)   Where a child is unable to "express specific, clear and consistent instructions but does express definite views or preference" counsel is obliged to communicate such views and preferences to the court and adduce evidence to establish those views;
(3)   Where the child's instructions, views or preferences, are in the mind of child's counsel contrary to the child's "best interests", such counsel is to act upon the child's instructions and to express the child's views, but in addition to advance to the court, counsel's own view of what is in the child's "best interests". The court considered that counsel for parents should be in no different position insofar as the manner upon which they represent parents.

Re J.C. and S.C. (1980), 31 O.R. (2d) 53, at p. 56 (Prov. Ct.).
"Where counsel has been appointed by the court to represent the children, that counsel has a responsibility to both the children and the court and I am not convinced that the judge should either remove counsel from the record or permit them to withdraw from the record in those circumstances where they feel compelled to act in the best interests of the child."

Re W. (1980), 27 O.R. (2d) 314, 13 R.F.L. (2d) 381 (Prov. Ct.).
In acting for a child in a welfare matter counsel should advance a child's wishes and preferences, presenting accurate and complete evidence which is consistent with the child's position.

Re T. and C.C.A.S. Metro. Toronto (1984), 46 O.R. (2d) 347, 39 R.F.L. (2d) 279 (Prov. Ct.).
In proceedings under the *Child Welfare Act* there are three reasons for holding that a parent does not have the absolute authority to retain counsel on behalf of a child. First, s. 20 recognizes that a child may have separate legal representation in child protection proceedings. Second, a child may have separate interests worthy of special protec-

tion in proceedings such as these. Third, major practical problems could arise if a separate lawyer for the child is not appointed until it has been determined that the child is in need of protection.

Re M. (1982), 29 C.P.C. 44 (Ont. Prov. Ct.).
Where there is a Crown wardship application of a newborn, on the basis that the mother is a schizophrenic, pre-trial discovery procedures are appropriate to allow child's counsel to prepare and to attempt to settle the application at an early stage.

SECTION 39. PARTIES AND NOTICE

This section: (1) stipulates who are the parties to a proceeding under Part III, and (2) prescribes the conditions under which they may participate. The rights of a child to participate and the circumstances in which they arise, are set out as well.

s. 39(1) The following are parties to a proceeding under this Part:
  1. The applicant.
  2. The society having jurisdiction in the matter.
  3. The child's parent.
  4. Where the child is an Indian or a native person, a representative chosen by the child's band or native community.

(2) At any stage in a proceeding under this Part, the court shall add a Director as a party on his or her application.

(3) Any person, including a foster parent, who has cared for the child continuously during the six months immediately before the hearing,
  (a) is entitled to the same notice of the proceeding as a party;
  (b) may be present at the hearing;
  (c) may be represented by a solicitor; and
  (d) may make submissions to the court,
  but shall take no further part in the hearing without leave of the court.

(4) A child twelve years of age or more who is the subject of a proceeding under this Part is entitled to receive notice of the proceeding and to be present at the hearing, unless the court is satisfied that being present at the hearing would cause the child emotional harm and orders that the child not receive notice of the proceeding and not be permitted to be present at the hearing.

(5) A child less than twelve years of age who is the subject of a proceeding under this Part is not entitled to receive notice of the proceeding or to be present at the hearing unless the court is satisfied that the child,

(a) is capable of understanding the hearing; and
(b) will not suffer emotional harm by being present at the hearing,
and orders that the child receive notice of the proceeding and be permitted to be present at the hearing.
(6) A child who is the applicant under subsection 60 (4) (status review), receives notice of a proceeding under this Part or has legal representation in a proceeding is entitled to participate in the proceeding and to appeal under section 65 as if he or she were a party.
(7) Where the court is satisfied that the time required for notice to a person might endanger the child's health or safety, the court may dispense with notice to that person.

The equivalent sections of the *Child Welfare Act* were fragmented throughout the Act.

COMMENTARY:

The objective of s. 39 is to set conditions defining those who are to be the parties to a proceeding; those who are to be entitled to receive notices, to be present at the hearing, and so on. Because it so completely governs input into the hearing, its impact is significant. As for those entitled to be the parties to the proceeding, they are identified clearly in s. 39(1). Section 39(1) is a new subsection. As it stands, it reflects an effort to clarify a number of ambiguities which existed in the old law on the matter of party status and other rights of persons with interest in the hearings.

1. Party Status and the Right to Notice

Party status is important to anyone at the hearing. It ensures that such person has legal status under the Act, generally,

(1) to commence proceedings;
(2) to receive notice of proceedings;
(3) to call witnesses at a proceeding;
(4) to examine witnesses at a proceeding,
(5) to make representations; and
(6) to be accorded other ancillary rights under the Act and under court rules.

Party status carries such privileges under all of Part III whether the proceeding is by way of protection, access status review or other proceedings.

It is clear from s. 39(1) that not all persons likely to be interested in a hearing are classed as parties to the hearing. The positions of three such persons are covered in s. 39 of the Act, and these are looked at below. They are: (1) A Director, (2) A foster parent, and (3) The child who is the subject of the proceedings.

(i) *A Director:*   Section 39(2) provides that, on an application from a Director, the court must add such Director as a party. This subsection is new. Under the *Child Welfare Act* the Director had status to be heard at a hearing. Such right was afforded in respect of any protection application and any access and status review application. Nothing however, was clearly stipulated in the Director's favour, as in this section of the new Act.

(ii) *The foster parent:*   Under s. 39(3), the person who has been the foster parent for the previous six months (or any other person who has cared for the child for that period), is entitled to notice, to presence, to counsel, and to make submissions. This ensures at least the opportunity for such person's position to be advanced, though no further participation is allowed. The foster parent is neither a party to the hearing nor accorded the right to call evidence or examine witnesses. This applies in respect of protection, access, and status review proceedings.

The predecessor section to s. 39(3) for protection applications in the *Child Welfare Act*, was spread among a number of subsections, including s. 28(3), (6) and (8). Subsections (3) and (6) dealt with notice and disposition relative to foster parents. The rights, beyond notice, afforded to a foster parent, were specified in s. 28(8). These were the right to make representations to the court and be represented by counsel. Also, for the old Act's provisions on access applications, see s. 35; for status review on society wardship, see s. 37; and for status review on Crown wardship, see s. 38. The new Act has clearly done some needed tidying-up.

It is of note that there was no definition of "foster parent" under the old Act. Indeed, the new Act provides only tenuous guidance at s. 3(1) 14., where the term is indirectly defined as having a "corresponding meaning" to foster care.

(iii) *The child who is the subject of the proceeding:*   Perhaps most noteworthy in the conferral of party status is one that stands out by its absence. In almost all instances, the child is not a party to the proceedings. In fact only where the child is an applicant would party status apply. Even where a child commences a status review under s. 60(4), the child appears at best to have a pseudo-party status in the proceedings (see s. 39(6) ". . . is entitled to participate in the proceedings and to appeal under s. 65 *as if he or she were a party.*"). However, where a child is the applicant on an access application (see s. 54(2)) party status would appear to be conferred.

This does not mean that the child is totally excluded from the proceedings. Section 39(4) and (5), as seen above, define the child's rights in this respect. These, however, are limited to having notice and being present at the hearing. Furthermore, both these rights are circumscribed. A child 12 years old or more is entitled to notice and presence, *unless* the court is satisfied that the hearing would cause emotional harm. A child *under* 12 is not entitled to notice and presence *unless* the court is satisfied the child would understand the hearing and would not suffer emotional harm. The application is broad, so as to apply to any proceeding under Part III of which the child is subject.

(a) *Child 12 or over:*   Let us first consider s. 39(4), concerning a child 12 or over. Comparing this with s. 28(7)(a) of the old law, we see that that section addressed only the matter of notice. The essence of its wording was repeated in several other *Child Welfare Act* sections; s. 32(7)(a), s. 37(4)(a), s. 38(4)(a) covering Status Review on Supervision, Access Applications, and Status Review on Society Wardships respectively. Section 39(4) of the new Act replaces all these sections.

As seen, those dealt only with *notice*. The matter of a child's *presence* at a hearing was covered in an entirely different section of the *Child Welfare Act,* namely s. 33(a). The court would decide whether or not the child should be excluded. Any such order would start from the presumption of a child's right to be present unless the court were satisfied that the hearing would injure the child's emotional health.

In the new Act the age at which the child would be entitled to notice and presence, is raised from ten to 12. But the possible danger of emotional harm remains as a factor precluding notice to a child 12 years or over. And if the court determines that such harm would be caused, the stipulated order is "that the child not receive the notice . . . and not be permitted to be present".

Missing in s. 39(4) is any direction as to which individual or party has an obligation to put the matter before the court. Further, the section does not offer any guideline concerning the type or quality of evidence which would be sufficient for a court to determine "emotional harm" to a child resulting from the child's possible presence at a hearing. Presumably, if such evidence is to support depriving a child of notice and presence at a hearing, it would have to be weighty and serious. A report from a doctor, psychologist or psychiatrist would seem to be a routine requirement.

Finally, it would appear that considerable flexibility will be needed in relating the applicability of the section to the child's age. Suppose an eleven-year-old is apprehended whose 12th birthday intervenes before the date of hearing. In this case it is suggested that the section should operate in the child's favour and he or she should be permitted at the hearing.

(b) *Child under 12 years of age:* Section 39(5), concerns the rights of notice and presence for a child under 12 years. This subsection also consolidates a number of predecessor provisions under the *Child Welfare Act.* It replaces s. 28(7)(b), which denies *notice* to a child under ten unless the child is entitled to be *present* under clause 33(b). Presence, under this clause, is also denied to the child unless the court is satisfied that the hearing would be understandable to the child and not injurious to the child's emotional health.

The position of the old law was, then, that notice and presence for an under-age child were prohibited, except when two specified tests had been passed:

(1)   such child had the capacity to understand the proceeding; and
(2)   such child would suffer no emotional harm from being present.

Thus the criteria and their application have not changed between the old and new laws. Permitting notice and presence for the (under-age) child still requires a positive step by a court. A motion with affidavit material made up of expert psychiatric, psychological and medical evidence of sufficient weight to deflect a court's concerns over the child's emotional stability would be an imperative.

As distinct from s. 39(4), however, the matter of emotional ability to cope is only one of two ingredients in s. 39(5). The court must be satisfied that the capability to understand exists in the child. It seems to be implied that there is a need to show that the child can understand:

(1)   the nature of the proceeding;
(2)   the consequences that may result from such proceeding.

Such a motion would presumably be advanced by counsel appointed by or for the child. Given the increase of the age from ten to 12 years, it may well be that the proportion of total cases where such applications would be satisfied, will increase.

Since the old Act had no general section relative to notice to a child, but inserted sections throughout Part II, the new subsection likewise replaces s. 32(7)(b) (Status Review on Supervision), s. 35(5)(b) (Access Applications), s. 37(4)(b) (Status Review on Society Wardship) and s. 38(4)(a) (Status Review on Crown Wardship).

S. 39(6): The Child Who Applies For Status Review

Section 39(6) is new. It defines those circumstances where a child is entitled to participate in the proceeding "as if he or she were a party", thus going well beyond the rights of notice and presence. Participation by a child, however, is limited to three circumstances, namely:

1.   where the child is an applicant for status review under s. 60(4) which requires that such child be twelve years or older; or

2.   where the child has received notice, which matter would be governed by the conditions of s. 39(4) and (5) and would in all likelihood result in such child being twelve years or older; or

3.   where the child has legal representation in a proceeding.

Points 1 and 2 are straightforward and seem consistent with the rest of the Act. In most cases included under 1 and 2, the child will be at least 12 years old; and if less than 12, the child will have been deemed by the court to be capable of understanding the hearing. This cannot be said, however, for point 3. The child for whom legal representation is afforded need not be over 12, and need not satisfy any test of capability of understanding; yet it would appear from a plain reading of the section that such child is entitled to participate "as if he or she were a party". Thus some questions are left open. Does s. 39(6) provide the guarantee? In practice it seems likely that the child under 12 will continue to be prohibited from court unless so ordered, and his participating right will continue to be assumed by counsel. Section 35(6) should be read concomitantly with s. 35(5).

Further, the section is unhelpful in providing meaning for "participate". Is the right to participate the equivalent of party status? If so, why is the child not simply identified as a party in all cases? Common sense would dictate that its plain meaning should prevail. Participation seems to imply the right to do all of the things that a party can do as enumerated above.

Where the child is within the category defined in s. 39(6) the right to "participate" applies equally to the appeal resulting from any such proceeding.

S. 39(7) Dispensing With Notice:

This subsection allows the court to dispense with notice to any person, if the time required for notice might endanger the child's health or safety. The subsection addresses itself to "person", which must be construed as referring to any persons, described in the section, as being eligible to receive notice. Those include the "parties" to a proceeding who are listed in s. 39(1) – the applicant, the society, the parent, the band or native community representative. Additionally, it must include persons in s. 39(3) (foster parents), and, under restricted circumstances, the child in s. 39(4).

As it stands, s. 39(7) is not tied to any other subsection, as was its predecessor. In the *Child Welfare Act*, s. 28(10) provided that where notice, required under s. 28(6), could not be effected and might therefore endanger the health or safety of the child, the court might dispense with the notice requirement. In that Act, the persons who were to receive notice (subject to s. 28(11)) were identified as:

(1)   the parent or other person having actual custody of the child;

(2)   the foster parent who immediately prior to the hearing had cared for the child over a period of at least six months; and

(3)   where applicable, the child.

The old provision applied to the matter of supervision, society and Crown wardship, status reviews and access applications with necessary modifications as a result of the application of s. 28(16). The new provision, on the other hand, applies to *any* proceeding under Part III of the Act.

The test however, remains the same: that delay for service might endanger the child's health or safety. Such test is not light or trivial and must be the subject of proof. Most instances, under the *Child Welfare Act* involved proceeding with a show cause subsequent to an apprehension where the whereabouts of both parents are unknown. However, for the purposes of a hearing a court has not generally in the past dispensed lightly with the right of a parent to notice. Indeed, such applications have in the past been tempered by the proviso conditions of the *Child Welfare Act* s. 28(11).

Section 40. COMMENCING CHILD PROTECTION PROCEEDINGS

The purposes of this section, which includes 17 subsections, are principally:

(i)   to establish the right of a society which believes a child to be in need of protection, to apply for a court determination as to whether that child is in fact in need of protection; and

(ii) to provide for the safety of such child through his or her removal to a "place of safety", or return to a place of safety in cases where the child has left such a place without proper consent.

Many of the subsections have as their purpose to ensure that the child's removal or return to a place of safety is accomplished both effectively and expeditiously.

s. 40(1) Application

(1)   **A society may apply to the court to determine whether a child is in need of protection.**

COMMENTARY:

This subsection is new. Nowhere in the old Act is there any provision setting out as clearly as does s. 40(1), the authority of the Children's Aid Society. It is in this simple statement that the mandate of a Children's Aid Society to have the issue of protection judicially determined, rests.

S. 40(2): Warrant to Apprehend a Child

(2) A justice of the peace who is satisfied on the basis of a child protection worker's sworn information that,

(a) there are reasonable and probable grounds to believe that a child is in need of protection; or

(b) a child actually or apparently under the age of sixteen years has left or been removed from a society's lawful care and custody without its consent,

may, where he or she is also satisfied on the basis of the information that there are reasonable and probable grounds to believe that a less restrictive course of action is not available or will not protect the child adequately, issue a warrant authorizing a child protection worker to bring the child to a place of safety.

The equivalent section in the *Child Welfare Act* was s. 22(1).

COMMENTARY:

The subsection is considerably more restrictive than its predecessor in the *Child Welfare Act*. To be noted in particular, is the requirement of a warrant issued by a justice of the peace, on the basis of the sworn information of a child protection worker, before a child may be apprehended. The right of a child protection worker to apprehend a child without a warrant is strictly limited to a case where the time required to obtain a warrant poses a substantial risk to the child's health or safety. (See s. 40(6) *infra*)

Under the *Child Welfare Act*, on the other hand, a child could be the subject of protection proceedings where the child was apprehended without a warrant. A child under 16 years who was in the lawful care of a society and departed, could be similarly apprehended. (See s. 21(1) and (2) of the *Child Welfare Act*).

To apply to obtain a warrant under s. 40(2) of the new Act, an application must be brought before a justice of the peace, containing the sworn information of a child protection worker. It must establish as its ingredients:

(i) the reasonable and probable grounds upon which to believe the child to be in need of protection; or

   (ii) that a child under sixteen years had been the subject of an order or agreement in the society's favour, placing the child under the society's care and control, and that such child had departed or been taken without the society's consent; and

  (iii) that on reasonable and probable grounds a less restrictive course of action is not available or will not adequately protect the child.

For the child protection worker bringing such an application, the ingredients of the Act imply certain crucial steps. The information put before a justice of the peace must be specific and particular. The facts forming the basis for protection must be detailed with sufficient particularity as to date, time, place, identification of persons, events and incidents. The information of professionals such as doctors, psychologists or others should be cited wherever available. These data are essential to strengthen the basis for the conclusion that there are reasonable and probable grounds to believe that the child is in need of protection.

Where the child is already in the care of a society, the basis of such custody, in the form of an agreement under s. 29 (temporary care agreements) or an order under Part III, must be made out. A copy of such agreement or order should be appended to any documentation presented to the justice of the peace.

Finally, the justice of the peace must be satisfied that the issuance of a warrant is required, there being no less restrictive course available under which the child will be adequately protected. This will require that the child protection worker address the matter of alternative remedies. This is perhaps more critical in respect of a child not already within the protection procedure. A worker should address each of the less restrictive remedies as provided under Part II including:

(a)   temporary care agreements (s. 29);
(b)   special needs agreements (s. 30);
(c)   counselling (s. 28)

Where the worker is convinced that none of these is appropriate, the rationale for such a conviction must be made out. It is the general thrust of the Act that the least restrictive course be taken to ensure the protection of a child and the child's best interests. Those who must decide the ultimate course of action, will require satisfaction that the less restrictive options be shown as inappropriate. The onus of demonstrating the reasons will fall upon the worker.

Such proceedings are without notice to any person. Where such a warrant is issued, the worker will bring the child to a "place of safety", as defined in s. 37(1)(e).

S. 40(3): Order to Produce or Apprehend a Child

(3)   Where the court is satisfied, on a person's application upon notice to a society, that there are reasonable and probable grounds to believe that,

(a)   a child is in need of protection, the matter has been reported to the society, the society has not made an application under subsection (1), and no child protection worker has sought a warrant under subsection (2) or apprehended the child under subsection (6); and

(b)   the child cannot be protected adequately otherwise than by being brought before the court,

the court may order,

(c)   that the person having charge of the child produce him or her before the court at the time and place named in the order for a hearing under subsection 43(1) to determine whether he or she is in need of protection; or

(d)   where the court is satisfied that an order under clause (c) would not protect the child adequately, that a child protection worker employed by the society bring the child to a place of safety.

The equivalent subsection of the *Child Welfare Act* was s. 22(2).

COMMENTARY:

This subsection preserves the right of a third party (any person other than a Children's Aid person) to seek the commencement of court process to determine protection of a child. Such person must continue to take certain steps which require that:

(i)   an application be made to court;

(ii)   the application be on notice to a society;

(iii)   the application show facts needed to demonstrate, on reasonable and probable grounds, that a child is in need of protection;

(iv)   such facts have been reported to the society;

(v)   the society has, despite the reporting of such facts, taken no steps toward commencement of an application under subsection (1) or sought a warrant, under subsection (2) or apprehended the child under subsection (6).

(vi)   the child cannot be adequately protected otherwise.

When, from all the above, the court is satisfied that adequate protection requires that the child be brought before the court, the court then has two options:

(1)   to direct, by an order to produce, that the person having charge of the child, bring the child before the court;

(2)   if the court deems that (1) would not protect the child adequately, direct a child protection worker to bring the child to a place of safety.

There are similarities between the old and the new subsections here. The predecessor section was s. 22(2) of the *Child Welfare Act*, which lists similar requirements to those above, and provides for an application brought by "any person". One difference appears to be that, in the old law, the court could make an order in this case only "after affording the society an opportunity to be heard". This requirement is now dropped. Acting on the application, the court could:

(1)   order the society to detain the child in a place of safety; or
(2)   order a person in whose charge the child is, to produce the child before a court.

In the new law, a society still has the opportunity to state its position before a court, being entitled to receive notice of any such application. Interestingly, the priority of a court's remedies seems to have been reversed between the two laws. The court is now required to consider first the appropriateness of an order to produce; and only where this is seen by the court as not likely to protect the child adequately, to issue a warrant for a society worker to apprehend.

CASE LAW S. 40(3)

Re T. and C.C.A.S. Metro. Toronto (1984), 46 O.R. (2d) 347, 39 R.F.L. (2d) 279 (Ont. Prov. Ct.).
The order to produce provision of s. 21(1)(b) does not violate the *Charter of Rights and Freedoms* insofar as they relate to the parents' rights. The order to produce is that of the child, not the parent. It is only an order that the child be produced and nothing more; thus there is little, if any interference with a parent's rights. Also, the order to produce provides an opportunity for the parent to be heard at that time.

S. 40(4): Child's Name Not Required

(4)   It is not necessary, in an application under subsection (1), a warrant under subsection (2) or an order made under subsection (3), to describe the child by name.

The equivalent subsection under the *Child Welfare Act* was s. 22(4).

COMMENTARY:

This subsection is quite straightforward and makes abundant good sense. It is not uncommon in an investigation:

(a)   that a child's full and complete name is not known; even when the surname is known, it is often accompanied only by a nickname;

(b)   that in the protection investigation's first stages, birth verification has not been received by a society;

The technical requirement of a full and proper name is simply too onerous at this early stage. Moreover the obligation remains upon the society to have available the child's proper name and age before a court can make a protection finding (see s. 43(2)(a)).

S. 40(5): Authority to Enter

(5)   **A child protection worker authorized to bring a child to a place of safety by a warrant issued under subsection (2) or an order made under clause (3)(d) may at any time enter the premises specified in the warrant or order, by force if necessary, and may search for and remove the child.**

The equivalent subsection under the *Child Welfare Act* was s. 22(3).

COMMENTARY:

With minor modification the effect remains the same. The new subsection gives a child protection worker authority to enter, search for and to take into custody a child, the subject of a direction (whether by warrant or order) of a court. Such power is essential if the worker is to effectively discharge responsibilities for the protection of children. It is, in fact, further enhanced by the presence of subsections (7) and (16) in the current section.

S. 40(6): Apprehension Without Warrant

(6)   **A child protection worker who believes on reasonable and probable grounds that,**
      (a)   a child,
             (i)   is in need of protection, or
             (ii) is actually or apparently under the age of sixteen years and has left or been removed from a society's lawful care and custody without its consent; and
      (b)   there would be a substantial risk to the child's health or safety during the time necessary to bring the matter on for a hearing under subsection 43(1) or obtain a warrant under subsection (2),
      may without a warrant bring the child to a place of safety.

This new subsection combines portions of subsections (1)(a) and (2) of s. 21 of the *Child Welfare Act.*

COMMENTARY:

The thrust of the new Act is in the first instance, to require a child protection worker to seek a warrant under s. 40(2). That, however, does not ignore the reality that in certain defined circumstances, apprehension without warrant may be the only way by which the interests of a child can be appropriately safeguarded. In such special cases, not only must the child protection worker have reasonable and probable grounds to believe that a child is in need of protection; there must also be "a substantial risk to the child's health and safety" during the delay period. The weight of the test is increased in light of the use of the words "and" between clauses (a) and (b), and of "substantial risk" in (b).

There is no definition of the meaning or degree which is to be attached to the term "substantial risk". However, it has already a place in the definition of protection, having figured in the list of protection criteria at s. 37(2), appearing in clauses (b), (d) and (g). As an adjective, "substantial" confers upon "risk" a particular significance. *The Shorter Oxford English Dictionary* defines "substantial", in part, as follows:

1. that is, or exists as, a substance; having a real existence; subsisting by itself;
2. constitutes or involves an essential part, point, or feature; essential, material;
3. of real worth, reliability or repute;
4. having substance: not imaginary, unreal or apparent only; true, solid, real.

Allegations of risk based on unreliable or untested secondary sources or on speculation would fall quite short of "substantial risk". The motivation of the legislators was clearly to limit the circumstances where apprehension without warrant would be condoned, while allowing for that inevitable possibility.

To sum up, the Act appears to direct the child protection worker to recognize always that the preferred course under the law involves the use of a warrant under s. 40(2). That makes the issues reasonably straightforward and if the justice of the peace is satisfied that protection is needed and no less restrictive course of action is available, a warrant is issued. In the case contemplated by s. 40(6), the worker is at the frontier of the decision with few guidelines except those considered above. The only real way to make such a decision, as uncertain as one might feel in doing so, is to make it as though a justice of the peace were considering a warrant application.

S. 40(7): Police Assistance

(7) A child protection worker acting under this section may call for the assistance of a peace officer.

There was no equivalent subsection of the *Child Welfare Act.*

COMMENTARY:

This subsection is new. It applies equally to circumstances where a child protection worker acts upon:

(a) a warrant under s. 40(2);
(b) an order under s. 40(3); or
(c) an apprehension without warrant under s. 40(6).

It sanctions the actions of a peace officer who provides assistance in the task of bringing a child into care. This can be of particular significance relative to an apprehension without warrant.

However, the subsection provides no guidelines whatever to such peace officer, to help in his or her determination that assistance is appropriate. Perhaps, by its absence, the legislation is suggesting that this need not be of concern to an officer, since such person is afforded the protection of subsection (16) of s. 40.

S. 40(8): Consent to Examine Child

(8) A child protection worker acting under subsection (6) or under a warrant issued under subsection (2) or an order made under clause (3) (d) may authorize the child's medical examination where a parent's consent would otherwise be required.

There was no equivalent subsection in the *Child Welfare Act.*

COMMENTARY:

This subsection is new and was clearly needed. There was under the *Child Welfare Act* no provision dealing with the matter of consent for a medical examination. Indeed a perusal of the *Child Welfare Act* s. 21(1)(a), s. 22(1) and (2) shows it permitted under specified circumstances, that a child be taken from a parent or other person and delivered to a "place of safety" unless a court otherwise directed. The absence of any medical reference placed health care providers, including doctors and nurses, in a delicate situation. The dilemma for such persons was in fact clearly heightened in cases where medical examination was necessary to add substance to the evidence upon which apprehension was based.

Note that the new subsection addresses the matter of a "medical examination" only. A child protection worker bringing a child into care, in the absence of a court order, cannot authorize anything beyond an examination. Authorization for treatment of any type, would not appear to be included.

Only after the court has determined within a proceeding pending final determination, that a child is to remain in the temporary care of a society, will the society have clear authority to provide consent to medical treatment beyond an examination. (see s. 47(4)). This may be modified within an order reserving a parent's rights to consent to medical treatment. (see s. 58, concerning medical treatment of the child).

A society, in respect of a society or Crown ward, has greater latitude (subject to specified exceptions) to consent to medical treatment. (see ss. 58 and 59 of the new Act).

CASE LAW: S. 40(8)

Re A. and C.A.S. Metro. Toronto (1982), 141 D.L.R. (3d) 111 (Ont. Prov. Ct.).
An apprehension of a child places a society in the position of parent and, accordingly, it can authorize medical treatment, before a protection finding is made.

S. 40(9): Place of Open Temporary Detention

(9)   Where a child protection worker who brings a child to a place of safety under this section believes on reasonable and probable grounds that no less restrictive course of action is feasible, the child may be detained in a place of safety that is a place of open temporary detention as defined in Part IV (Young Offenders).

There was no equivalent subsection in the *Child Welfare Act.*

COMMENTARY:

This subsection is new. Under it, the child protection worker bringing a child to a place of safety – with a warrant under subsection 40(2), or without warrant under subsection 40(6) – may detain the child in a place of open temporary detention as defined in Part IV. (see s. 84(g)). The worker's justification for such action must be that the worker "believes on reasonable and probable grounds that no less restrictive course of action is feasible."

A "place of safety" has already been defined at s. 37(1)(e), to exclude a place of secure custody or a place of secure temporary detention as defined in Part IV. However, an open temporary detention program is defined (in s. 85(2)(b)), as one "in which restrictions that are less stringent than in a secure temporary detention program are imposed on the liberty of young persons."

In making the decision to detain a child in a place of open temporary detention, the worker should be particularly sensitive to the proviso that "no less restrictive course of action is feasible." This would be especially so if the child is under the age of 12 years.

The definition of "young person" in Part IV (Young Offenders) at s. 84(n) is confined to children between 12 and 16 years of age, and it is primarily these children that are placed in open temporary detention. Exposure of a child under 12 years of age to such children may be seen to be not in that child's best interest.

Such questions may in fact be answered through the authority to make regulations at s. 200(1)(a), under which the Lieutenant Governor in Council may make regulations for the purposes of Part IV:

(a)   governing the establishment, operation, maintenance, management and use of places of temporary detention, open custody and secure custody and other services and programs provided under subsection 85(1).

Conceivably, such regulations may ensure safeguards for children under 12 years of age who are placed in open temporary detention.

Perhaps the most reassuring aspect is the length of time such child may be detained in a place of temporary open detention. Section 42(2) provides that:

Within twenty-four hours after a child is brought to a place of safety that is a place of open temporary detention, or as soon thereafter as is practicable, the matter shall be brought before a court for a hearing under section 43(1) . . .

Even though the section provides that, subject to there being no less restrictive course of action feasible, the child may remain in such temporary open detention for up to 30 days (s. 42(2)), the conditions of such detention may be expected to receive some critical review at the hearing.

S. 40(10): Apprehension of Child Under Twelve

(10)   A peace officer who believes on reasonable and probable grounds that a child actually or apparently under twelve years of age has committed an act in respect of which a person twelve years of age or older could be found guilty of an offence may apprehend the child without a warrant and shall, on doing so,

(a)   as soon as practicable, return the child to the child's

parent or other person having charge of the child; or

**(b)   where it is not possible to return the child to the parent
or other person within a reasonable time, take the child
to a place of safety to be detained there until the child
can be returned to the parent or other person.**

There was no equivalent subsection in the *Child Welfare Act.*

COMMENTARY:

With the enactment of the *Young Offenders Act* S.C. 1980-81-82-83, c.
110 persons under 12 years of age who may otherwise have been the
subject of proceedings under the *Juvenile Delinquents Act* R.S.C.
1970, c. J-3 for offences, are now *not* the subject of proceedings under
federal legislation. Such children may be the subject of proceedings
under the *Child and Family Services Act* by virtue of the protection
definition at s. 37(2)(j) and (k).

This subsection, for which there is no *Child Welfare Act* predecessor, is directed at the peace officer.

The subsection gives no clue as to the meaning to be ascribed to
the word "offence." Is it to be restricted to any "offence" as defined at
s. 2(1) of the *Young Offenders Act* S.C. 1980-81-82-83, c. 110? Is it to
include an "offence" as defined by provincial or municipal authority? Aside from such questions, however, the section permits a peace
officer to apprehend without warrant and then deliver the child to
the custodial person or to a place of safety until the custodial person
can again take charge of the child.

S. 40(11): Notice to Parent

**(11)   The person in charge of a place of safety in which a child is
detained under subsection (10) shall make reasonable efforts
to notify the child's parent or other person having charge of
the child of the child's detention so that the child may be
returned to the parent or other person.**

There was no equivalent subsection in the *Child Welfare Act.*

COMMENTARY:

This subsection is new. It is connected to subsection (10) of s. 40 and is
a straightforward obligation upon the person having charge of the
place of safety to which the child is delivered.

S. 40(12): Where Child Not Returned to Parent etc. Within Twelve Hours

**(12)   Where a child detained in a place of safety under subsection
(10) cannot be returned to the child's parent or other person
having charge of the child within twelve hours of being**

taken to the place of safety, the child shall be deemed to have
been apprehended under subclause (6)(a)(i) as being apparently in need of protection.

There was no equivalent subsection in the *Child Welfare Act.*

COMMENTARY:

This subsection is new. Its provisions accentuate the importance of
the task falling upon the person having charge of the place of safety
under subsection (11).

S. 40(13): Apprehension of Child Absent from Place of Open Temporary Detention

(13)   Where a child is detained under this Part in a place of safety
that has been designated as a place of open temporary detention as defined in Part IV (Young Offenders) and leaves the
place without the consent of,
(a)   the society having care, custody and control of the
child; or
(b)   the person in charge of the place of safety,
a peace officer, the person in charge of the place of safety or
that person's delegate may apprehend the child without a
warrant and,
(c)   take the child to a place of safety to be detained until he
or she can be returned;
(d)   arrange for the child to be returned; or
(e)   return the child,
to the first-mentioned place of safety.

A similar provision was contained at s. 21(2) and s. 22(1)(b) of the
Child Welfare Act.

COMMENTARY:

This subsection is new. It appears to deal only with a child who leaves
a place of open temporary detention. In this sense, it complements
the provisions of subsection (6)(a)(ii), which covers other instances of
a child leaving the care of a society. In both cases, the intent is to
ensure the ability to act swiftly to re-apprehend a child, by providing
that such action may be taken without a warrant. In the current
subsection, it is to be noted that the child need not be returned
immediately to the original place of open temporary detention; interim placement in some other place of safety is permitted, provided
that the ultimate destination is the original place.

The subsection bears some similarity to the provisions of s. 21(2) and s. 22(1)(b) of the *Child Welfare Act*. However it provides for the return of a child leaving a place of open temporary detention, to that place by:

(a) a peace officer; or
(b) the person in charge of the place of safety or that person's delegate,

without a warrant. The similarity is closer to the provisions of s. 21(2) of the *Child Welfare Act* as opposed to s. 22(2) which required a warrant.

S. 40(14): Right of Entry

> (14) Where a person authorized under subsection (6), (10) or (13) believes on reasonable and probable grounds that a child referred to in the relevant subsection is on any premises, the person may without a warrant enter the premises, by force, if necessary, and search for and remove the child.

COMMENTARY:

This subsection re-enforces the three foregoing subsections of s. 40(6), (10) and (13) in which provision is already made for apprehension of a child without warrant. It will be recalled that these subsections provided respectively as follows:

(6) apprehension by a child protection worker,
(10) apprehension by a peace officer, and
(13) apprehension by a peace officer or by a person in charge of a place of open temporary detention.

The provision sanctions entry onto any premises, by force if necessary, provided that the objective is to "search for and remove the child." Subsection (14) does not constitute the authority for the apprehension of the child; it is the authority to enter premises in order to search for a child, and its effect is that a search warrant in the regular sense is unnecessary.

Similar provisions were found under the *Child Welfare Act*, in particular at ss. 21(3) and 22(3).

S. 40(15): Regulations Re: Power of Entry

> (15) A person authorized to enter premises under subsection (5) or (14) shall exercise the power of entry in accordance with the regulations.

There was no equivalent subsection in the *Child Welfare Act*.

COMMENTARY:

This subsection is new. Regulations for entry upon premises under the *Child Welfare Act* did not exist. The authority to promulgate such regulations is pursuant to s. 199(a) which provides:

> **s. 199 The Lieutenant Governor in Council may make regulations for the purposes of Part III,**
>
> **(a) governing the exercise of the powers of entry set out in subsections 40(5) and (14).**

S. 40(16): Protection From Personal Liability

> **(16) No action shall be instituted against a child protection worker or peace officer for any act done in accordance with this section, unless the act is done maliciously or without reasonable grounds.**

There was no equivalent subsection in the *Child Welfare Act*.

COMMENTARY:

This subsection is new. It provides, within the limits prescribed, protection for:

(i) the child protection worker; and

(ii) the peace officer,

that the *Child Welfare Act* never addressed.

It should be noted that subsection (16) does not address the liability of either of these persons to charges under the Criminal Code, which might be initiated by:

(i) a child;

(ii) a parent or other person in whose custody a child might be;

(iii) the Attorney General or any Crown Attorney on his or her behalf.

S. 40(17): Powers of Peace Officer

> **(17) A peace officer has the powers of a child protection worker for the purpose of this section.**

COMMENTARY:

Under the *Child Welfare Act*, s. 21(1) provided for a "police officer" to effect an apprehension. The use of this term was scattered about the subsections of ss. 21 and 22 of the old Act. Under the new Act, by virtue of the present subsection, the application is more consistent.

Thus the peace officer has the authority to:

(a)   enter premises without a warrant in search of a child (s. 40(5) and (14));

(b)   apprehend a child without a warrant subject to conditions (s. 40(6));

(c)   authorize a child's medical examination subject to conditions (s. 40(8));

(d)   detain a child at a place of open temporary detention under specified conditions (s. 40(9));

SECTION 41. HEARINGS AND ORDERS

The purpose of s. 41, which consists of ten subsections, is principally to protect the child against any possible adverse consequences of publicity which might be generated by a court hearing.

S. 41(1): Definition of Media

(1)   **In this section, "media" means the press, radio and television media.**

The equivalent subsections in the *Child Welfare Act* were s. 57(4) and (5).

COMMENTARY:

This subsection defines at the outside the scope of the word "media" and the group it may encompass. Its wording was used in the above-mentioned subsections of the *Child Welfare Act.*

S. 41(2): Application

(2)   **This section applies to hearings held under this Part, except hearings under section 72 (child abuse register).**

COMMENTARY:

This subsection is new; but only within the procedures of the new Act. It specifically excludes hearings related to the Child Abuse Register. For a discussion on hearings related to the Child Abuse Register, see s. 72, *infra.*

S. 41(3): Hearings Separate from Criminal Proceedings

(3)   **A hearing shall be held separately from hearings in criminal proceedings.**

A similar provision was contained in s. 57(1) of the *Child Welfare Act.*

COMMENTARY:

The intent here is to ensure as little contact as possible between persons accused in criminal proceedings, and children. This is similar to the previous intent of the *Child Welfare Act*, s. 57(1). Perhaps the new formulation is more "economical" in its focus, having dropped the specific (and somewhat narrow) restriction on the use of premises "ordinarily used for hearings in criminal proceedings." The word "separately" seems to accomplish the desired intent without the inflexibility that was built into the previous Act.

S. 41(4), (5), (6) and (7): Private Hearing unless Otherwise Ordered

(4)   A hearing shall be held in the absence of the public, subject to subsection (5), unless the court, after considering,
    (a)   the wishes and interests of the parties; and
    (b)   whether the presence of the public would cause emotional harm to a child who is a witness at or a participant in the hearing or is the subject of the proceeding,
    orders that the hearing be held in public.

(5)   Media representatives chosen in accordance with subsection (6) may be present at a hearing that is held in the absence of the public, unless the court makes an order excluding them under subsection (7).

(6)   The media representatives who may be present at a hearing that is held in the absence of the public shall be chosen as follows:
    1.   The media representatives in attendance shall choose not more than two persons from among themselves.
    2.   Where the media representatives in attendance are unable to agree on a choice of persons, the court may choose not more than two media representatives who may be present at the hearing.
    3.   The court may permit additional media representatives to be present at the hearing.

(7)   The court may make an order,
    (a)   excluding a particular media representative from all or part of a hearing;
    (b)   excluding all media representatives from all or a part of a hearing; or
    (c)   prohibiting the publication of a report of the hearing or a specified part of the hearing,
where the court is of the opinion that the presence of the media representative or representatives or the publication of the report, as the case may be, would cause emotional harm to a child who is a witness at or a participant in the hearing or is the subject of the proceeding.

The equivalent subsections of the *Child Welfare Act* were s. 57(2), (4), (5) and (6).

COMMENTARY:

Subsections (4) to (7) inclusive are interrelated. It is useful, therefore, to consider them together.

Two questions dominate these subsections: (i) Who may be present at hearings? ("The public" and "the media" are dealt with separately). (ii) What criteria are to be used to decide who may be present? (In particular, the effect on the child is considered).

(i) *Who may attend at hearings:* Subsections (4) and (5) provide that the public may *not* be present at hearings unless expressly given such a right by the court; and that the media, within limits, may attend, unless expressly denied such right by the court. These provisions are generally parallel to those found in the earlier legislation, with minor differences. Where the new legislation refers to "the public", for example, the *Child Welfare Act* (s. 57(2), (4), (5) and (6)) cited "all persons", as being excluded from a hearing. As for media representation, both the old and the new Acts were alike, providing as follows:

(i) that the media representatives who are permitted to attend may select two from amongst themselves where their number exceeds two;

(ii) where media representatives are unable to so agree then the court shall determine from amongst their number;

(iii) the presence of more than two of the media may be permitted by the court;

(iv) that the court may exclude media representatives from the whole or any part;

(ii) *Criteria for deciding who may attend hearings:* In the case of both the public and the media, the principal criterion is the possibility of emotional harm to any child involved in the hearing, whether that child be a witness, a participant or the subject of the proceeding. It is of note that this is a considerable widening of the application of the criterion of emotional harm. In the *Child Welfare Act*, s. 57(2), that criterion applied only to "any child who is present at the hearing." In the new Act, whether a child is present or not is immaterial. If the hearing deals with a child in such way as to make a child the "subject" of it, the criteria are broadened to include possible harm to such child. Thus the new Act is broader and more definitive in its application to the question of attendance, both of the public and of the media. The additional criterion to be considered by the court is "the wishes and interests of the parties." This is identical to the previous provision; despite the reference to the interests of the parties, the "best interests" test related to the child is not specifically cited.

Two general observations are in order. First, the new section is lacking (as was the old) in specifying with any particularity:

(a)   the relative weights to be accorded to the factors in (a) and (b) of s. 41(4);

(b)   the manner in which a court should exercise the discretion it has.

Further, the new Act requires (as did the old) the demonstration of some injury or harm to the emotional health of the child. This would normally require some measure of proof by way of an expert opinion that some psychiatric or psychological harm might result. It is possible that further uncertainty may be found to result from the change in wording – from "would be injurious to the emotional health" of a child (in the *Child Welfare Act*), to "would cause emotional harm to a child" (in the 1985 Act). The latter would seem to be a wider formulation, including short-term emotional upsets and their effects on a child's behaviour, as well as long-term injury to emotional health.

S. 41(8): Publishing Identity of Child

(8)   **No person shall publish or make public information that has the effect of identifying a child who is a witness at or a participant in a hearing or the subject of a proceeding, or the child's parent or foster parent or a member of the child's family.**

The equivalent section of the *Child Welfare Act* was s. 57(7)(a) and (b).

COMMENTARY:

As in the preceding subsections, the significant change here is the inclusion of a child who is "the subject of a proceeding", thus considerably widening the predecessor provision which referred only to a child "present at the proceedings." The new provision ensures against identification of any child, whether a witness or not, and whether present at the hearing or not, and whether the subject of a proceeding or not. One question which is still not clarified, however, is the following: Is such prohibition applicable in respect of the name of a child disclosed during testimony where the child is neither the subject of the proceeding, nor a witness or participant?

S. 41(9): Publicity Identifying a Person

    (9)   **The court may make an order prohibiting the publication of information that has the effect of identifying a person charged with an offence under this Part.**

The equivalent provision of the *Child Welfare Act* was at s. 57(7)(b).

COMMENTARY:

The previous legislation prohibited publication. The new legislation allows publication unless the court orders otherwise. This applies in respect of an "offence under this Part" (meaning Part III), and thus includes offences under ss. 75, 79, 80 and 81.

S. 41(10): Transcripts of a Hearing

    (10)   **No person except a party or a party's solicitor shall be given a copy of a transcript of the hearing, unless the court orders otherwise.**

There was no equivalent provision in the *Child Welfare Act*.

COMMENTARY:

This subsection is new. Its intent is clear. In order to control and to diminish the possibilities of information about any proceeding under Part III being disseminated, such a condition is imposed.

    The issue then becomes the circumstances under which a court would order the release of a transcript to any other person. Will the matter of public interest be raised? What weight would be attached to the public interest, given consideration of the Declaration of Principles at s. 1 of the Act? Will a court permit such an order with conditions prohibiting the disclosure of information that would be identifying in nature of the parties and persons involved? This might become particularly important where a proceeding involves matters of protection arising out of a child's conduct under circumstances outlined in s. 37(2)(j) and (k), where the child has killed or injured persons or damaged property.

    Since the child is not stipulated as a party to a proceeding at s. 39(1), it would appear that neither the child nor his or her counsel is entitled to obtain a copy of a transcript. Notwithstanding this, it seems likely that past practice will continue, and that the child's solicitors will be accorded the same rights in respect of the receipt of the transcript, as if he or she were a solicitor for a party.

SECTION 42. TIME FOR DETENTION LIMITED

The purpose of s. 42, which contains two subsections, is to place clear limits on the time during which a child, who has been taken to a place of safety, may be detained in such place. For this purpose, in the second subsection separate treatment is given to "a place of safety that is a place of open temporary detention."

S. 42(1)

  (1) **As soon as practicable, but in any event within five days after a child is brought to a place of safety under section 40 or subsection 75(6) or a homemaker remains or is placed on premises under subsection 74(2),**

      (a) the matter shall be brought before a court for a hearing under subsection 43(1) (child protection hearing);

      (b) the child shall be returned to the person who last had charge of the child or, where there is an order for the child's custody that is enforceable in Ontario, to the person entitled to custody under the order; or

      (c) a temporary care agreement shall be made under subsection 29(1) of Part II (Voluntary Access to Services).

The equivalent provision in the *Child Welfare Act* was at s. 27(1).

COMMENTARY:

In summary, subsection (1) provides that where a child has been:

(a) apprehended or otherwise taken from the person having care of the child;

(b) the subject of care by a homemaker,

such child must, within five days be the subject of:

(a) a court proceeding; or
(b) a return to a specified person; or
(c) a temporary care agreement.

The provisions are the subject of very little change from those of the *Child Welfare Act.*

CASE LAW: S. 42(1)

Re G. et al. (1978), 30 R.F.L. 224 (N.B. S.C.).
Where a child is apprehended but not for purposes of an interim placement order delivered before a court within a specified period of time as prescribed by statute, the court is not deprived of jurisdiction. The section of the statute presenting the requirement is *directory* only. (s. 27(1)).

Warnock v. Garrigan (1979), 8 B.C.L.R. 26, 6 R.F.L. (2d) 181 (C.A.).
Proceedings involving the protection of children are essentially civil
proceedings and hence the standard of proof is not that proof be
beyond a reasonable doubt. (s. 28(4)).

Caldwell v. C.A.S. of Metro. Toronto (1976), 27 R.F.L. 259 (Ont. Prov.
Ct.).
The onus upon the applicant Children's Aid Society is a civil one. But
in that it affects the rights of parent and child the onus is "very
demanding". (s. 28(1)).

S. 42(2): Place of Open Temporary Detention

(2)   Within twenty-four hours after a child is brought to a place
of safety that is a place of open temporary detention, or as
soon thereafter as is practicable, the matter shall be brought
before a court for a hearing under subsection 43(1) (child
protection hearing), and the court shall,
  (a)   where it is satisfied that no less restrictive course of
  action is feasible, order that the child remain in the
  place of open temporary detention for a period or periods not exceeding an aggregate of thirty days and then
  to be returned to the care and custody of the society;
  (b)   order that the child be discharged from the place of
  open temporary detention and returned to the care and
  custody of the society; or
  (c)   make an order under subsection 47(2) (temporary care
  and custody).

The equivalent provision in the *Child Welfare Act* was at s. 27(2).

COMMENTARY:

This subsection deals with the case of a place of safety which is a
place of open detention. It will apply, for example, where a child
protection worker detains a child under s. 40(9). It would appear to
apply as well where a child is returned to such a placement, having
departed under circumstances described at s. 40(13).

   Such a child must be brought before a court within 24 hours or
"as soon thereafter as is practicable" following the child's delivery to
such place. This is a significant distinction. In circumstances involving other "places of safety", the time for delivery before the court is
up to five days, (s. 42(1)(a)), and in the meantime there is the option of
returning the child to the person who last had charge or who is
entitled to custody, or of a temporary care arrangement, (s. 42(1)(b),
(c)). Under the present subsection (2) there is no alternative to bringing the matter before the court. Moreover, the much shorter time in

this subsection highlights the seriousness with which placement in open detention is regarded under the law.

The old observation and detention home provided under s. 27(2) of the *Child Welfare Act,* has given way to the place of open detention.

The court itself may determine, among a number of options, the issue of continued open detention or other placement of the child. The new Act provides a court with very little guidance on the issue. Under clause (a) of subsection (2), a court must be satisfied that "no less restrictive course of action is feasible", but there is neither a definition within the Act nor any help in determining the meaning or scope of this test. The importance which the legislators attach to this phrase is reflected in its inclusion in the Declaration of Principles at s. 1(c).

Where a court is satisfied as to the absence of a feasible alternative, continued placement at open detention may be sanctioned for a period up to 30 days. Thereafter a child must be returned to a society. Where a court considers that open detention is not appropriate, the child will be placed with a society, parents or other person, as described in s. 47(2).

The open detention placement then is limited in time. There appears to be no placement of a detention nature where the period may exceed 30 days in respect of proceedings under Part III.

SECTION 43. CHILD PROTECTION HEARING

The purpose of this section is to provide for a protection hearing and to establish certain ground rules which must be observed prior to a court's determining whether a child is in need of protection.

S. 43(1) and (2): Child's Name, Age, etc.

(1) Where an application is made under subsection 40(1) to determine whether the child is in need of protection, the court shall hold a hearing to determine the issue and make an order under section 53.

(2) As soon as practicable, and in any event before determining whether a child is in need of protection, the court shall determine,
  (a) the child's name and age;
  (b) the religious faith, if any, in which the child is being raised;
  (c) whether the child is an Indian or a native person and, if so, the child's band or native community; and
  (d) where the child was brought to a place of safety before the hearing, the location of the place from which the child was removed.

The equivalent provision in the *Child Welfare Act* was at s. 28(1).

COMMENTARY:

Subsection (1) provides for a court hearing to determine whether need for protection exists and to make a disposition order. Such hearing must follow an application made by a society under s. 40(1). A protection hearing is one consequence of the removal of a child to a place of safety under s. 42.

   Subsection (2) directs the court to make certain specific findings of fact, *prior to* a determination of the need for protection. These relate to the child's name and date of birth, religious affiliation, and the place from which a child was taken to any place of safety. The determination of these matters by a court is mandatory. Indeed, a court is obligated to make such determination, regardless of the disposition on the protection. This is in contrast with the requirement under the *Child Welfare Act* s. 28(1) where such findings were only required in the event of a determination that protection was needed.

   A more significant departure in the new legislation is the requirement in s. 43(2)(c), that the court determine whether a child is an Indian or native person. This reflects the "best interests" criterion contained in s. 37(3) 3., and s. 37(4). It also helps to ensure the complete identification of parties to the hearing, with particular reference to parties described at s. 39(1) 4. Finally, it gives effect to one of the purposes of the Act, as enunciated at s. 1(f):

> **to recognize that Indian and native people should be entitled to provide, wherever possible, their own child and family services, and that all services to Indian and native children and families should be provided in a manner that recognizes their culture, heritage and traditions and the concept of the extended family.**

CASE LAW: S. 43(1) and (2):

Re H. and C.A.S. Kenora (1983), 19 A.C.W.S. (2d) 330 (Ont. Prov. Ct.). Once a society has commenced an application for protection the court must hold a hearing. Thus society request to withdraw the application was refused.

R.C.C.A.S. Essex and Warren (1983), 44 O.R. (2d) 283, 37 R.F.L. (2d) 322 (Co. Ct.).
See s. 37 above. (old s. 19).

Re C.A.S. Metro Toronto and C. (1979), 25 O.R. (2d) 234 (Prov. Ct.). See s. 37(2) above. (old s. 19).

Forsyth v. C.A.S. of Kingston and County of Frontenac, [1963] 1 O.R. 49, 35 D.L.R. (2d) 690 (H.C.J.).

On application seeking *certiorari* to quash a temporary order for society wardship as the result of a "Hearing" conducted at a hospital shortly after the child's birth, the child of parents who were Jehovah's Witnesses was in need of a blood transfusion for which neither parent was prepared to consent. Participants, inclusive of a Family Court Judge, representatives of the Children's Aid and hospital staff, along with the parents convened at the hospital. The court directed that the order should be quashed on the basis that a true and meaningful "Hearing" had not been conducted. The language of Rose C.J.H.C. was adopted from *Re Fairfield Modern Dairy Ltd. and the Milk Control Board of Ont.*, [1942] O.W.N. 579 at 582: "A hearing is a real hearing at which the charge is made known, the evidence in support of it is adduced, the supposed offender is given an opportunity of meeting that evidence by cross-examination or by the calling of witnesses, or otherwise, as may be requisite, and it is against all ordinary principles of the administration of justice to call anything less than that a hearing". The elements of a hearing included notice; an explanation to the parents of their rights where they had no counsel nor opportunity to engage counsel; the opportunity to examine witnesses and to call evidence.

S. 43(3): Where Sixteenth Birthday Intervenes

(3) **Despite anything else in this Part, where the child was under the age of sixteen years when the proceeding was commenced or when the child was apprehended, the court may hear and determine the matter and make an order under this Part as if the child were still under the age of sixteen years.**

There was no equivalent provision in the *Child Welfare Act.*

COMMENTARY:

This subsection is new. Under the provisions of s. 19(1) of the *Child Welfare Act,* a child 16 years of age or older who had not already been the subject of some order under Part II of that Act was beyond the scope of that legislation. That position is continued under the *Child and Family Services Act* by virtue of the definition of "child" at s. 37(1)(a). However, the legislature intended that a child who was the subject of court proceedings under Part III, and who was under 16 years at the moment of commencement or apprehension, should remain under the court's jurisdiction, even after the 16th birthday. For example, a child apprehended May 14th whose 16th birthday was May 15th, would still remain within the jurisdiction of the court despite the show-cause proceeding being held after the 16th birthday.

The subsection confers a discretion upon the court as to whether it will hear an application under those circumstances. However, it gives no direction on how, when, or on what basis such discretion is to be exercised.

CASE LAW: S. 43(3):

R. v. Allcock (1977), 25 R.F.L. 84 (B.C. S.C.).
A child who was apprehended while still under 17 years of age was over that age at the time of her appearance before a judge. On appeal the court found that the trial judge had no jurisdiction. The requirement upon which the court might deal with the child was that the child had to have been less than 17 years of age at the time of apprehension and at the time of the court appearance.

SECTION 44. JURISDICTION

The purpose of s. 44, which includes four subsections, is to establish rules to determine where a hearing will be held, in terms of the "territorial jurisdiction" of a society, and the conditions under which a proceeding may be transferred. It also places a territorial restriction on an order made by a court.

S. 44(1): Definition of Territorial Jurisdiction

(1)   In this section, "territorial jurisdiction" means a society's territorial jurisdiction under subsection 15(2).

There was no equivalent provision in the *Child Welfare Act.*

COMMENTARY:

While the *Child Welfare Act* addressed the matter of proceedings transferred at s. 19(3), it did not give clear and concise guidelines on the matter of a society's territorial jurisdiction, or of the significance of such jurisdiction on the geographical location of the appropriate court.
    This section flows from the provisions of s. 15(2) of the new Act which provides:

(2)   The Minister may designate an approved agency as a children's aid society for a specified territorial jurisdiction and for any or all of the functions set out in subsection (3), may impose terms and conditions on a designation and may vary, remove or amend the terms and conditions or impose new

terms and conditions at any time, and may at any time amend a designation to provide that the society is no longer designated for a particular function set out in subsection (3) or to alter the society's territorial jurisdiction.

S. 44(2): Place of Hearing

(2)   A hearing under this Part with respect to a child shall be held in the territorial jurisdiction in which the child ordinarily resides, except that,

    (a)   where the child is brought to a place of safety before the hearing, the hearing shall be held in the territorial jurisdiction in which the place from which the child was removed is located;

    (b)   where the child is in a society's care under an order for society or Crown wardship under section 53, the hearing shall be held in the society's territorial jurisdiction; and

    (c)   where the child is the subject of an order for society supervision under section 53, the hearing may be held in the society's territorial jurisdiction or in the territorial jurisdiction in which the parent or other person with whom the child is placed resides.

The equivalent provision in the *Child Welfare Act,* was at s. 19(2).

COMMENTARY:

This subsection sets out the rules for the location of any hearing under Part III. These are that the child will normally be dealt with by the court in the place of the child's "ordinary residence" with three exceptions:

	Circumstance	Place of Hearing
(a)	The child is brought to a place of safety before the hearing,	the territorial jurisdiction of the place from which the child was removed.
(b)	The child is in a society's care under an order for society or Crown wardship under s. 53,	in the society's territorial jurisdiction.
(c)	The child is the subject of an order of supervision under s. 53,	in the supervising society's territorial jurisdiction OR the place where the child resides.

    This gives further meaning to the determination which the court is required to make under s. 43(2).

S. 44(3): Transfer of Proceeding

(3)   **Where the court is satisfied at any stage of a proceeding under this Part that there is a preponderance of convenience in favour of conducting it in another territorial jurisdiction, the court may order that the proceeding be transferred to that other territorial jurisdiction and be continued as if it had been commenced there.**

The equivalent provision in the *Child Welfare Act* was at s. 19(3).

COMMENTARY:

While the basic rules as to the jurisdiction of a court are stipulated in s. 44(2), circumstances may arise which dictate a transfer to a place which might not on its face appear consistent with these rules. Under s. 44(3) court has the leeway to effect such a transfer. This section would be the authority upon which a court could choose between the two alternatives presented in s. 44(2)(c) on the review of the supervision order.

A significant difference between the new and the old Acts is the court's right under s. 44(3) to make a transfer determination at "any stage of the proceeding." This is much broader than the more restrictive condition of s. 19(3) "at any time after an application is made . . . and before hearing the application . ."

CASE LAW S. 44(3)

Re P. (1982), 36 O.R. (2d) 324 (Prov. Ct.).
An application for status review may be transferred to a court of another county or district where the preponderance of convenience would be served to do so.

S. 44(4): Court Order and Society's Territorial Jurisdiction

(4)   **The court shall not make an order placing a child in the care or under the supervision of a society unless the place where the court sits is within the society's territorial jurisdiction.**

The equivalent provision in the *Child Welfare Act* was at s. 30(1), paragraphs 1. and 2.

COMMENTARY:

The significance of the subsection is clear: a court shall place a child only in the care of a society in whose territorial jurisdiction the court sits.

This limitation may cause difficulties for parties to a proceeding. For example, the evidence at a hearing may disclose that there are family members who are suitable caregivers for a child, but that they reside outside of the society's jurisdiction. The court entertaining the application has no jurisdiction to specify those family members as the custodians of the child. The only solution is to transfer the proceedings under s. 44(3) on the basis of "preponderance of convenience."

SECTION 45. POWERS OF COURT

This section specifies the powers of the court to compel attendance of witnesses, testimony and documentation.

> **The court may, on its own initiative, summon a person to attend before it, testify and produce any document or thing, and may enforce obedience to the summons as if it had been issued under the *Family Law Reform Act* R.S.O. 1980, c. 152.**

The equivalent provision of the *Child Welfare Act* was at s. 28(2).

COMMENTARY:

Section 45 makes clear that a court may, without the request of a party, conduct its own inquiry through the powers of:

(a)   summoning a person to attend;
(b)   requiring the production of any document or thing; and
(c)   enforcing the summons through use of the *Family Law Reform Act* R.S.O. 1980, c. 152 contempt provisions or its successor legislation.

This section raises numerous questions:

(1)   who is to examine the witness in chief?
(2)   which party is able to cross-examine the witness?
(3)   must the provisions of the *Evidence Act* R.S.O. 1980, c. 145 be complied with before documents can be introduced into evidence as records or reports?

This section is unique to the extent that it abrogates the general principle that the applicant is in control of deciding what evidence will be called (Dominus Litis). To an extent, the exercise of these powers removes the judge from the position of adjudicator to that of litigant. The court, in effect, descends into the forum of the parties. Presumably, this power is justified as part of the paternalistic attitude often utilized in proceedings involving children.

SECTION 46. EVIDENCE AT HEARING

This section covers the type of evidence admissible at hearings, and the order of its presentation.

> **(1)** Despite anything in the *Evidence Act,* before ordering that a child be placed in or returned to the care and custody of a person other than a society, the court may consider that person's past conduct toward any child that is or has been in his or her care, and any oral or written statement or report that the court considers relevant, including a transcript, exhibit or finding in an earlier civil or criminal proceeding, may be admitted into evidence and shall be proved as the court directs.

The equivalent provision in the *Child Welfare Act* was at s. 28(4).

COMMENTARY:

This subsection permits a court to admit for consideration, evidence about a person's past conduct toward any child. Free from the restrictions that might otherwise be imposed by the *Evidence Act,* (though not completely by-passing rules as to admissibility, given the authority to direct the manner in which it may be admitted), such evidence may include:

  (i) oral statements;
 (ii) written statements;
(iii) reports;
 (iv) transcripts;
  (v) exhibits;
 (vi) findings.
in any earlier civil or criminal proceeding.

The statements made to police or other authorities resulting subsequently in a civil or criminal proceeding involving an abuse to a child, appear to be contemplated by this subsection.

Reference to the body of caselaw already developed under s. 28(4) will provide some assistance as to the manner in which courts have directed the admission of such evidence.

S. 46(2): Order of Presentation of Evidence

> **(2)** In a hearing under subsection 43(1) evidence relating only to the disposition of the matter shall not be admitted before the court has determined that the child is in need of protection.

There was no equivalent provision in the *Child Welfare Act.*

COMMENTARY:

On first reading it would appear to contrast with much present practice, where the applicant, the Children's Aid Society, in the past would frequently present before a court, all of its evidence at one time. Such evidence would touch upon not only the issue of protection, but as well the "best interest test", which would be determinative of the matter of disposition.

On first blush the provisions of s. 46(2) would seem to dictate that in the hearing of a s. 43(1) application, there would be a two-tier proceeding. Such tiers would include the first stage – making out the matter of "protection" – and thereafter the second stage – determining, under the "best interests test", which disposition should be ordered under s. 53 of the Act.

Support for this approach can be inferred from s. 43(1) itself, which states in part, ". . . the court shall hold a hearing to determine the issue and make an order under section 53." Strictly speaking, only when a protection determination has been made in the affirmative, can the court move to the disposition stage under s. 53. That section reads in part" . . . Where the court finds that a child is in need of protection and is satisfied that intervention through a court order is necessary to protect the child in the future, the court shall make one of the following orders, in the child's best interest . . ."

Further support is found in s. 52, to be examined later. The society is required, under the provisions of s. 52 to prepare for the court's use, a plan in writing for the child's care. Such plan must address itself almost exclusively to the disposition of the case *on the assumption that a need for protection has already been found to exist.* The court is required to obtain and consider this plan "before making an order [for disposition] under s. 53 or 61." From this it is clear that the society's plan could not be readily admitted into evidence prior to the protection finding having been made.

The practical consequences of the application of a two-tier system are numerous. Witnesses giving evidence as to the matter of protection may find themselves being called a second time, being the subject of an examination-in-chief, cross-examination and re-examination on evidence already given, as to disposition under "the best interest" test. In addition, trials may become more protracted and lengthy, resulting in delays in dispositions, which may give rise in the mind of a court to conflict over the best interests criteria, especially that at s. 37(3), paragraph 10: "the effects on the child of delay in the disposition of the case." On the other hand, with evidence limited to the protection issue, where no need for protection is found, the hearing will be considerably shorter.

One purpose of the section may well be to protect people; the reason being that, unless the court does find that protection of the child is necessary, and thus has to make an order for disposition, the presentation of such evidence would be gratuitous and irrelevant, and likely in some cases, prejudicial to a party.

However, there may be some different interpretation as to the two-tier theory in this connection. Firstly, the provision carefully restricts itself to ". . . evidence relating *only* to the disposition of the matter . . .". This may be interpreted to mean that evidence of a mixed character touching upon both the matter of protection and disposition, could be introduced during the protection issue stage. Such an interpretation would certainly lessen the number of instances where evidence would have to be shunted to the second stage of a proceeding.

In addition, given a further examination of s. 46(2) and of the words ". . . shall not be *admitted* before the court has determined . . ." may permit a court to have such evidence *presented* and thereafter determine its admissibility, once a protection finding has been made. Again, as a result, evidence as to disposition only could be presented during the course of the protection-finding stage of the trial and admitted formally by a judge's order at the time that the trial entered the disposition stage, if in fact, a protection finding had been made.

All such comments have ultimately to be considered against the hard reality that built-in delays and backlogged court dockets, and continued strain on the time of judges across the province, make the courts reluctant to generously interpret a section which only further taxes an already over-burdened system. [Emphasis added in preceding quotations.]

CASE LAW: S. 46(2):

St. Pierre and Meloche et al. v. R.C.C.A.S. for Essex County (1977), 27 R.F.L. 266 (Ont. Div. Ct.).
The appellants argued that the evidence as to disposition and protection was admitted and was considered at the same time and prior to any protection finding. It was argued that evidence as to disposition should not have been considered by the trial judge until the issue of protection had been determined. After a review of the Act then existing (where there was no equivalent s. 46(2) provision under the *Child and Family Services Act*), Holland J. stated, at p. 270: "We are of the view however, that there is nothing to prevent the judge from hearing all of the evidence dealing with both issues before the court at the same time."

D. v. C.A.S. of Kent County (1980), 18 R.F.L. (2d) 223 (Ont. Co. Ct.).
Any consideration of the type of s. 30 order sought by the applicant

prior to a determination of protection is inappropriate. The Society must first satisfy the heavy civil onus of demonstrating protection before any consideration of the type of s. 30 order is to be made.

SECTION 47. CONDITIONS FOR ADJOURNMENT OF A HEARING

This section provides for the conditions of an adjournment, including the temporary care needed for a child during an adjournment period.

S. 47(1): Time Limits on Adjournments

(1)   The court shall not adjourn a hearing for more than thirty days,
  (a)   unless all the parties present and the person who will be caring for the child during the adjournment consent; or
  (b)   if the court is aware that a party who is not present at the hearing objects to the longer adjournment.

The equivalent provision in the *Child Welfare Act* was at s. 28(13).

COMMENTARY:

Like its predecessor, the section provides that there shall be no adjournment of a hearing for more than 30 days *unless* the consents required under clause (a) are forthcoming, and the court is not aware of an objection from a party not present at the hearing.

This provision should not be construed as a direction that the trial or disposition of any proceeding under Part III must be completed within 30 days of commencement. Section 48 makes this clear. The current section means that the matter must come before the court at least every 30 days unless the required consents are provided. The evident intent is to ensure that matters involving the interests of children are not "lost in the shuffle"; and that the process of bringing these on for hearing is done with dispatch. It permits a judge the opportunity to probe and question any reasons for delay and exercise authority to speed the process.

Questions do arise on interpretation of s. 47(1). Where a Children's Aid Society brings a child into care, and institutes a foster home placement, is it the society or the foster parent that is the ". . . person who will be caring for the child . . ."? It is more likely that a court will interpret such "person" as being the society. Secondly, by what means will a person, who is not present and making an objection to a longer adjournment, have that considered by a court? Section 28(13) of the former Act made it plain that such objection had to be "in writing." Is that standard lessened by the broader wording of s. 47(1)(b)?

S. 47(2): Custody of Child During Adjournment

(2)   Where a hearing is adjourned, the court shall make a temporary order for care and custody providing that the child,

    (a)   remain in or be returned to the care and custody of the person who had charge of the child immediately before intervention under this Part;

    (b)   remain in or be returned to the care and custody of the person referred to in clause (a), subject to the society's supervision and on such reasonable terms and conditions relating to the child's supervision as the court considers appropriate;

    (c)   be placed in the care and custody of a person other than the person referred to in clause (a), with consent of that other person, subject to the society's supervision and on such reasonable terms and conditions relating to the child's supervision as the court considers appropriate; or

    (d)   remain or be placed in the care and custody of the society, but not be placed in,

        (i) a place of secure custody as defined in Part IV (Young Offenders), or

        (ii) a place of open temporary detention as defined in that Part that has not been designated as a place of safety.

The equivalent provision in the *Child Welfare Act* was at s. 28(12).

COMMENTARY:

Essentially, the court has the obligation, when any hearing is adjourned, to:

(a)   order the return of the child to the person from whom the child was taken, with or without society supervision;

(b)   direct the placement of the child with some third party under society supervision; or

(c)   direct that the child remain in the society's care subject to the restrictions in s. 47(2)(d)(i) and (ii) as to placement.

The new formulation is clearly more explicit than was its predecessor on the matter of the options before the court. Under the former Act, the court in devising an order upon adjournment was allowed some leeway in the following:

> **... unless the court is satisfied that some other order for care and custody of the child should be made, in which case, the court may make such other order for the temporary care and custody of the child as the court considers advisable pending final disposition...** (s. 28(12), *Child Welfare Act*).

The new subsection clearly permits a court to make what amounts to an interim order of supervision pending trial, for example the return of the child to a parent or other person under a society's supervision. Judges under the *Child Welfare Act* were most reluctant to consider interim supervision because of:

(i) lack of clear statutory direction sanctioning it;
(ii) concern that such an order might amount to a determination of "protection" and prejudice a "party or parent".

The language of the new Act expressly permits interim supervision.

The second difference is the use in s. 47(2)(a) of the words "remain in or be returned to the care and custody of the person who had charge of the child . . ." There may be some consideration that the use of the words, ". . . the person who had charge of the child immediately before intervention . . .", does not necessarily mean the person who had ". . . the care and custody . . ." of the child. There may be some argument that "the person" in s. 47(2)(a) could include a babysitter who had "charge" of the child (even though a transitory charge) pending the return of another person or parent. If such argument is considered valid, then the person to whom the child has to be returned would be the babysitter. Such an argument would have application to s. 47(2)(b) as well. Indeed, there are several other sections of the Act where a similar conundrum would arise.

However, the words ". . . remain in or be returned to the care and custody . . ." in s. 47(2)(a) would certainly seem to imply that something far greater than a transitory "charge" of the child on a temporary basis is meant. Otherwise, one might encounter the rather ludicrous situation where a babysitter has priority in terms of placement of a child rather than a parent or other person who had "care and custody" prior to intervention.

The terms "having care and custody" and "having charge", of a child, occur with some frequency in the Act, but the intended distinction between them is not made very clear. A rigid interpretation such as that above might lead to absurd results. Yet, in the absence of clear signals in the Act, the argument is not totally without logic.

This raises an important question. As they are used in this Act, are the two terms meant to imply the same thing? That is to say, are they meant to be interchangeable terms with identical meanings? If they are, the further question arises as to why *both* terms are used in juxtaposition throughout the Act. One can only conclude from the fact that they *are* so used, that a difference *is* intended.

What is the difference? Perhaps it could be at least partly explained as follows. The concept of having charge is akin to that of having responsibility. "Care and custody" *implies* "charge". The person who has care and custody of the child has responsibility for the child. That responsibility can be *shared* with another (a teacher, a babysitter), but one can never relinquish the responsibility without relinquishing the care and custody on which it rests.

Viewed from this perspective, the person who has "care and custody" of the child has at all times the charge (responsibility) of the child, whether at the moment such charge is being shared or not. Such an interpretation would rule out the possibility of a problem such as the foregoing. Nonetheless, more careful legislative definitions would unquestionably have helped.

Where a child is taken by a person, a court may consider interim placement with another person, provided such person consents to the placement. Grandparents, adult siblings or close relatives may most likely fall into this category of persons a court might consider.

The society obtaining an order that the child remain in its interim care is obliged to make placements subject to the restrictions imposed at s. 47(2)(d). "Secure custody" or "open temporary detention" are not permitted placements. This, it might be observed, is a carry-over from similar restrictions imposed under s. 28(12) of the *Child Welfare Act.*

There is an important difference between the *Child Welfare Act's* s. 28(12) and s. 47(2) of the new Act about the duration of a temporary placement order.

Under the *Child Welfare Act* provision s. 28(12) stated in part, "A court may from time to time adjourn a hearing . . . and pending final disposition of the hearing . . ." make a temporary placement order. The section stipulated that such an order once made, remained in effect until the hearing of the application. This was subject only to the provisions of s. 28(14) which permitted an application for variation of an order made under s. 28(12). As a result, in the absence of an application to vary, despite the reappearance of the matter any number of times before the court because of repeated adjournments, after the initial s. 28(12) order but before the hearing, the temporary order remained intact and escaped further review or inspection.

This is distinctly not the case under s. 47(2). The words ". . . pending final disposition of the hearing . . ." have given way to language which states, "Where a hearing is adjourned, the court shall make a temporary order for care and custody . . ." This would seem to mean that any order for temporary placement made upon a first adjournment, would be scrutinized by the court under the guidelines of s. 47(2) on each occasion of a subsequent adjournment. However, there is some thinking that the exclusion of those words does not deprive a judge of the authority to make such an order pending "hearing".

In addition, given the s. 28(14) *Child Welfare Act* counterpart at s. 47(6), permitting variation of such temporary orders, variation of temporary placement could be considered quite frequently by a court, between the first appearance in court and hearing.

In light of the foregoing and in particular the fact that on each occasion of adjournment, the issue of temporary placement may well be re-litigated, it seems unlikely that any respondent would make much use of s. 47(6). In addition, given the need to examine temporary placement on every adjournment, the risk is that matters will become lengthier and more protracted.

CASE LAW: S. 47(2):

Re C.C.A.S. Metro. Toronto and G. (1984), 47 O.R. (2d) 504 (Prov. Ct.). The ordinary focus of a show cause hearing is a determination of the likelihood of *substantial risk of harm* to the child if returned to the custody, care and control of a parent. If full disclosure of the society's case is not provided then the appropriate course of action would be to request the missing information from the society and if it is not forthcoming then move under Rule 20 for examination.

S. 47(3): Criteria For Custody During Adjournment

(3)   The court shall not make an order under clause (2)(c) or (d) unless the court is satisfied that there are reasonable and probable grounds to believe that there is a substantial risk to the child's health or safety and that the child can not be protected adequately by an order under clause (2)(a) or (b)

There was no equivalent provision in the *Child Welfare Act*.

COMMENTARY:

This subsection establishes the criteria upon which a court should select an interim placement elsewhere than the custody of the person who had charge prior to intervention. A child must be returned to the person who had charge of the child unless:

(a)   there are reasonable and probable grounds of substantial risk to the child if returned; and

(b)   the child cannot adequately be protected if returned, even under society supervision.

Section 28(12) of the *Child Welfare Act* simply imposed an onus on the society to "show cause why the child should remain or should be placed" in its care. In the new law, the onus still rests upon the society, but the circumstances which the society must establish before removal of a child is permitted, are clarified and particularized.

The inclusion of the new section is very much in keeping with the Declaration of Principles of the new Act. In particular, it gives effect to the emphasis in s. 1, clauses (b) and (c), which recognize the need to support the "autonomy" and "integrity" of the "family unit", in the least restrictive or disruptive way. Thus children should be returned, with or without supervision, pending a full hearing of the matter on the merits, unless strong reasons are adduced to the contrary.

What in essence, is the obligation upon a society seeking to make an objection to return? It must make out what amounts to a *prima facie* case of "protection", as defined at s. 37(2). It must demonstrate "substantial risk" from which the child cannot be adequately protected, even with supervision, in the home from which the child was taken.

S. 47(4): Consent for Medical Treatment of a Child Under Society Care

(4)   **Where the court makes an order under clause (2)(d), section 58 (parental consents) applies with necessary modifications.**

There was no equivalent provision in the *Child Welfare Act.*

COMMENTARY:

This subsection is new. Where a child is in the care of a society during an adjournment, this subsection authorizes the society to consent to the medical treatment of a child. Under the *Child Welfare Act* there was no such authority conferred upon a children's aid society for a child in its interim placement. Such authority appeared to be conferred only under an order *actually* made in its favour for Crown or society wardship (see s. 40 and 41 of the *Child Welfare Act*).

Such provision, however, applies only in the event of placement in the care of a society. Return of the child to the person from whom the child was taken or to any third person, does not trigger the application of the section. In addition, the court may, under s. 58 as applied to adjournments, order that the right to consent to or refuse medical treatment for the child, remain with the parent.

S. 47(5): Access During Adjournment

> (5) An order made under clause (2)(c) or (d) may contain provisions regarding any person's right of access to the child on such terms and conditions as the court considers appropriate.

A similar provision was in the *Child Welfare Act* at s. 28(12).

COMMENTARY:

This provision in a sense is new. It specifically empowers a court to direct access where a child is placed with a third person or in the care of a society. In addition a court may impose terms. These might specify hours, place, frequency, and whether such access is to be supervised.

The section is new in the sense that courts under an order directing temporary placement with a society under s. 28(12) of the *Child Welfare Act* would occasionally make provision for access in favour of a parent or other person; the term "access" appears nowhere in that subsection. Indeed it is absent from any part of s. 28.

To what extent may a court impose restrictions as to access? For instance, where the father-abuser is residing in the matrimonial home with the mother, to whom the court is inclined to consider giving the child on an interim supervisory placement: can the court direct the exclusion of the father from his own home and regulate his access to the child? Competing interests come into conflict: parental rights versus the best interests of a child and preservation of a family's integrity.

A judge of the Provincial Court (Family Division) has limited authority at best to make what could amount to an order of exclusive possession in favour of one spouse over another under the *Family Law Act 1986*, S.O. 1986, c. 4. However, there is no express power to so do under the *Child and Family Services Act*.

When a parent is unwilling to agree to such being excluded, it seems likely that a court lacking express and clear jurisdiction relative to interim placement, would direct the child to remain in care of a children's aid society.

This dilemma appears not to affect a court's powers to exclude a person from access with a child, once a protection finding is made, if the remedies of s. 76 are used.

S. 47(6): Variation of a Temporary Placement Order

> (6) The court may at any time vary or terminate an order made under subsection (2).

The equivalent provision in the *Child Welfare Act* was at s. 28(14).

COMMENTARY:

Any order made by a court as to temporary placement continues to be subject to variation or termination. However it is noteworthy that in s. 47(6) there has been a deletion of the test in s. 28(14), upon which a court made such variation or termination, namely: "... that cause has been shown why a change ... should be made ..." This is somewhat akin to the "material change in circumstances" test applied in maintenance cases dealt with by divorce and matrimonial legislation. In the absence of some such criterion, what indeed is to be the test?

S. 47(7): Admissibility of Evidence in Adjournment Proceedings

(7)   **For the purpose of this section, the court may admit and act on evidence that the court considers credible and trustworthy in the circumstances.**

The equivalent provision in the *Child Welfare Act* is at s. 28(15).

COMMENTARY

This provision permits the court to accept evidence, the quality of which would otherwise be rejected. Such evidence may be primarily "hearsay" and might for example, include information provided through the primary children's aid worker, such as:

(a)   the emergency admission record from a hospital;
(b)   a written report of a physician, psychologist or other professional;
(c)   a police occurrence or other report;
(d)   notes of attending after-hours or other children's aid employee;
(e)   affidavit evidence of any of the above.

The provision would, for interim proceedings under this section, allow the admission of such evidence notwithstanding the normal safeguards against it, including the notice sanctions under ss. 35 and 52 of the *Evidence Act* R.S.O. 1980, c. 145. Use of the word "may" confers upon the "court" the discretion as to whether such evidence will be allowed.

The subsection is limited. It applies only to the matter of adjournment and a child's placement pending a return to court. It is only within this context that such unique circumstance applies to the admissibility of evidence.

The predecessor subsection was most frequently relied upon in what have been termed "show cause" hearings, and this will probably continue. Within five days of the apprehension of a child, if the society feels that the child should be kept in its care, it must bring the application to court and demonstrate to the court's satisfaction that the child ought to remain so during a period of adjournment. The adjournment is often given to allow the parents to obtain counsel or for the setting of a pre-trial or trial date some time later.

Where a child has been apprehended by a society worker, the society may have evidence available from a neighbour of the child, an attending police officer, a society after-hours worker, a hospital emergency ward nurse and attending physician, and a society social worker. The court time available rarely allows for the evidence of all the above persons to be given. Thus, one person who has contacted or collected reports from the persons referred to above, can introduce that evidence, which will be of a "hearsay" nature.

CASE LAW: S. 47(7):

R. v. Allcock (1977), 25 R.F.L. 84 (B.C. S.C.).
While interpreting the age restrictions applicable to children the subject of proceedings before the court relative to their protection status, a court considered the standard of proof. In relying upon the dicta of *Re S.V.'s Infant* (1963), 43 W.W.R. 374 (B.C. Co. Ct.) the court concluded that since child protection legislation interfered with the subject it was in the nature of a criminal proceeding.

C.A.S. Dist. of Kenora and Paishk et al. (1985), 48 O.R. (2d) 591 (H.C.J.).
On a status review application to extend society wardship a court may make its decision on the basis of unsworn testimony and reports presented to the court on the basis of s. 28(4).

Re Family and Child Services of London and Middlesex and C. et al. (No. 2) (1982), 23 A.C.W.S. (2d) 282 (Ont. Prov. Ct.).
A transcript of a previous trial dealing with the parents' access in another trial was *not* admissible in a trial involving the same parents.

T.T. v. C.C.A.S. Metro. Toronto (1984), 42 R.F.L. (2d) 47 (Ont. Prov. Ct.).
Section 28(4) at most, confirms the discretion of the trial judge to avoid technical, borderline and otherwise unnecessary hearsay exclusions, if there are grounds and circumstances tending to guarantee reliability. That is the essential test for hearsay that comes from *Ares v. Venner*, [1970] S.C.R. 608, 12 C.R.N.S. 349, and s. 28(4) could certainly be read so as to dovetail with that test.

Re J.C. (1984), 39 R.F.L. (2d) 244. (Ont. Prov. Ct.)
The applicant society sought to introduce into evidence those parts of the respondent mother's hospital chart which contained opinions of

doctors and nurses as to the mother's parenting capacity. These opinions were formed by observing the mother's conduct in hospital immediately after the birth of the child that is the subject of these protection proceedings. It was the view of the court that s. 28(4) was enacted to make it clear that similar fact evidence as to the *past* parenting is admissible in child welfare proceedings. While it permits hearsay to be adduced, it should not be construed so as to enable the very conduct complained of to be proved by recorded hearsay in the absence of necessity or exceptional circumstances.

E.C. et al. v. C.C.A.S. Metro. Toronto (1982), 37 O.R. (2d) 82 (Co. Ct.); affg 21 R.F.L. (2d) 426 (Prov. Ct.).

At trial the court on a Crown wardship application permitted the Society to introduce under s. 28(4) the transcript evidence on a hearing which resulted in a Crown wardship order of a sibling to the child the subject of the instant proceeding. On appeal of the Crown wardship order an objection was taken to the admissibility of such transcript evidence. The court found that the language of s. 28(4) was broad enough to encompass the circumstances of the case and permit the admission of the transcripts. The court approved the dicta of Provincial Court associate chief Judge Walmsley in *C.A.S.Metro Toronto v. N.H.B., D.A.E.* (also known as D.A.B. and B.A.E. Sr.,) unreported May 8, 1980 where various documents relating to the care by the mother to children other than the child the subject of the proceeding were admitted. Walmsley Provincial Court Judge stated: "It will be seen that, by s. 28(4) the trial judge is given a very wide discretion: the material may be hearsay; it may be opinion; it may be mere speculation; nevertheless if it bears on the past conduct of a person to a child it is admissible." The section is applicable in any case where the child may be placed "in the custody of that person whose conduct is improved". The court referred to *Re Wanda S.,* (unreported September 23, 1980) a decision of Provincial Judge Felstiner who stated in reference to the application of s. 28(4): "I believe s. 28(10) means that because of the unique nature of child welfare matters with the heavy emphasis on ensuring that all pertinent information concerning a child will be put before the court, formal rules of procedure will be tempered by the need to have full disclosure to the court. In s. 28(2), (4) and (16) normal evidentiary rules have been relaxed for the same reason".

SECTION 48. DELAY – COURT TO FIX DATE

This section sets a three-month time limit on delays following an application to determine protection.

48.   Where an application is made under subsection 40(1) to determine whether a child is in need of protection and the determination has not been made within three months after the commencement of the proceeding, the court,

(a)   shall by order fix a date for the hearing of the application, and the date may be the earliest date that is compatible with the just disposition of the application; and

(b)   may give such directions and make such orders with respect to the proceedings as are just.

There was no equivalent provision in the *Child Welfare Act.*

COMMENTARY:

This section is new. The safeguards against lengthy adjournments provided in s. 47(1) do not ensure the fixing of a date for disposition by hearing, or otherwise, by a court. To carry through on the intent to promote "the best interests of a child" enunciated in s. 37(3), paragraphs 5., 7. and 10., the implementation of some safeguard was essential. Section 48, however, does not guarantee the fixing of an early date for hearing even after the lapse of three months. A court will naturally take into account all of its trial commitments under all the statutes over which it has jurisdiction. However, under this section it will be required to address the matter and to fix a date, all in the light of "the just disposition of the application".

By virtue of s. 48(b), a court may make whatever directions it considers appropriate. Such directions may include the setting of a pre-trial hearing date, the ordering of examinations, the establishment of the order of case presentation (*i.e.* the order of cross-examination by the several respondents), or the provision of counsel for a child, etc.

Finally, this is not the only piece of provincial legislation with such a provision. Under the provisions of s. 26 of the *Children's Law Reform Amendment Act,* S.O. 1982, c. 20 a similar provision applies in connection with a custody application commenced for which no disposition has been made within six months of its commencement. Likewise by s. 26(2) a court retains authority to "give such directions in respect of the proceedings . . . as the court considers appropriate."

This section appears to have no application to reviews under s. 60 and s. 61.

SECTION 49. COURT TO GIVE REASONS

This section requires a court to give the reasoning underlying an order under Part III, including the alternatives considered and the evidence presented.

49(1) Where the court makes an order under this Part, the court shall give,

    (a)   a statement of any terms or conditions imposed on the order;

    (b)   a statement of every plan for the child's care proposed to the court;

    (c)   a statement of the plan for the child's care that the court is applying in its decision; and

    (d)   reasons for its decision, including,

        (i)   a brief statement of the evidence on which the court bases its decision, and

        (ii)   where the order has the effect of removing or keeping the child from the care of the person who had charge of the child immediately before intervention under this Part, a statement of the reasons why the child cannot be adequately protected while in the person's care.

  (2) Clause (1)(b) does not require the court to identify a person with whom or a place where it is proposed that a child be placed for care and supervision.

This section consolidates a number of sections in the *Child Welfare Act*, principally s. 30(4) and (5) and s. 36.

COMMENTARY:

This provision will normally apply in the making of an order under s. 53 directing supervision, society or Crown wardship, or other possible disposition. By virtue of its wide scope, however, it would apply to other orders under Part III, including orders for:

(a)   legal representation for a child (s. 38(3));

(b)   protection or apprehension of a child (s. 40(3));

(c)   procedural determinations (e.g. s. 39(7) dispensing with notice);

(d)   exclusion of any persons (s. 41);

(e)   transfer of proceeding (s. 44(3));

(f)   adjournment and determination of placement (s. 47);

(g)   fixing of a date for hearing (s. 48);

(h)   assessments (s. 50);

(i)   access (ss. 54 and 55);

(j)   payment of maintenance (s. 56);

(k)   parental authority for medical consents (s. 58(1));

(l)   society authority for medical consents (s. 58(3));

(m)   review (ss. 60 and 61);

(n)   production of records (s. 70(3));

(o)   restraining any person (s. 76);

Certainly, not all of the statements called for in s. 49(1)(a) to (d) would be expected in most of the orders issued under Part III. The reasons called for under (1)(d)(i) would be expected in all of them, but the rest would be dependent on the individual circumstances.

By virtue of the definition of "court" in s. 3(1)(ii), restricting it to the Provincial Court (Family Division) or the Unified Family Court, the section would appear not to apply to orders of any District Court on appeal as permitted under s. 65; or the Supreme Court of Ontario for injunctive relief under s. 83.

This section provides a checklist for the court to adopt in the development of any order.

CASE LAW: S. 49:

C.A.S. Dist. of Kenora v. Paishk et al. (1985), 48 O.R. (2d) 591 (H.C.J.). The provisions of s. 36 (for which oral or written reasons should be provided for a decision made) are directory only and "failure to comply with all its terms would not cause a loss of jurisdiction."

SECTION 50. ASSESSMENTS

This section provides for professional assessments (medical, emotional, developmental, psychological, educational or social) of a child or parent and establishes ground-rules governing the use and disposition of the assessment report.

s. 50(1) and (2): Order For and Report of Assessment

(1)   Where a child has been found to be in need of protection, the court may order that within a specified time,
 (a)   the child; or
 (b)   a parent or a person, except a foster parent, in whose charge the child has been or may be,
attend before and undergo an assessment by a specified person who is qualified, in the court's opinion, to perform medical, emotional, developmental, psychological, educational or social assessments and has consented to perform the assessment.

(2)   The person performing an assessment under subsection (1) shall make a written report of the assessment to the court within the time specified in the order, which shall not be more than thirty days unless the court is of the opinion that a longer assessment period is necessary.

The equivalent provisions in the *Child Welfare Act* are at s. 29(1).

COMMENTARY:

Section 50 has eight subsections. The first two subsections address the matter of the order for assessment and the resulting report. It can be seen that these and the predecessor section share points of common ground:

   (i) that a court has the authority to order an assessment;

  (ii) that such assessment may *not* be ordered by a court until a child has been found to be "in need of protection";

 (iii) that a court may direct an assessment of:
    (a) any child; or
    (b) any person and in particular a parent (except a foster parent);
    (c) or both.

 (iv) that such assessment may be done by any person qualified in the court's opinion, to conduct a:
    (a) medical;
    (b) emotional;
    (c) developmental;
    (d) psychological;
    (e) educational; or
    (f) social
    assessment;

  (v) that any assessor considered must have consented to do the assessment;

 (vi) that the report of the assessor be in writing and submitted to the court within 30 days or such longer time as the court directs.

The provisions of s. 50 apply only to assessments as directed by order of the court and after a finding of "protection" has been made.

However, in many cases placed before the court, assessments of children and parents and other persons are done on a voluntary or consent basis as between the parties. While there is absolutely no authority to provide that such voluntary or consent assessments must be governed by s. 50, (nor were they governed by s. 29 of the *Child Welfare Act*) it seems likely that a judge of a court before whom such assessment is placed, would wish to check its consistency with the provisions of s. 50(1): principally three questions:

1.   was the assessor qualified?
2.   did the assessor consent to perform the assessment?
3.   were copies in a reasonable period of time provided to all other parties?

S. 50(3): Copies of Assessment Reports

(3)   At least seven days before the court considers the report at a hearing, the court or, where the assessment was requested by a party, that party shall provide a copy of the report to,

(a)   the person assessed, subject to subsections (4) and (5);

(b)   the child's solicitor or agent of record;

(c)   a parent appearing at the hearing, or the parent's solicitor of record;

(d)   the society caring for or supervising the child;

(e)   a Director, where he or she requests a copy;

(f)   where the child is an Indian or a native person, a representative chosen by the child's band or native community; and

(g)   any other person who, in the opinion of the court, should receive a copy of the report for the purposes of the case.

The equivalent subsection of the *Child Welfare Act* was s. 29(2).

COMMENTARY:

The persons listed as entitled to a copy of the report are essentially the same in this and the predecessor Act. The only new player is the representative of the child's band or native community where the child is an Indian or native person. The only significant difference is the obligation on the court (where the court has ordered the assessment), or on the party which requested the report, to serve it at least seven days before the hearing. The absence of such a time period in s. 29(3) of the *Child Welfare Act* made service with short notice a distinct possibility and could have resulted in a person entitled to the report being surprised or ill-prepared. Furthermore, by virtue of the fact that such report constituted part of the record under s. 29(4), service of it just before or during the hearing would deprive a party of the opportunity to subpoena the assessor for purposes of examination on the content of the report.

Where the court, without a request of a party, orders an assessment, upon whom does the obligation to provide a copy of the report to the individuals listed in (a) through (g) rest? Does the clerk of the court obtain the report and then serve it on the relevant individuals at least seven days before the court is to consider it?

The subsection indicates that where a party requests a report, that party is required to provide it to the enumerated individuals. Does this apply to voluntary assessments or only to court-ordered assessments, where the order was made at the request of a party? A requesting party is not going to get copies of the report for distribution, (because only the court is going to get these for distribution). This phrase therefore appears meaningless.

S. 50(4) and (5): Child's Access to Report

(4)   Where the person assessed is a child less than twelve years of age, the child shall not receive a copy of the report unless the court considers it desirable that the child receive a copy of the report.

(5)   Where the person assessed is a child twelve years of age or more, the child shall receive a copy of the report, except that where the court is satisfied that disclosure of all or part of the report to the child would cause the child emotional harm, the court may withhold all or part of the report from the child.

The equivalent provision of the *Child Welfare Act* was at s. 29(3).

COMMENTARY:

These pertain to delivery of a copy of the assessment to a child, the subject of the assessment. A child under 12 years will not normally receive a copy unless the court considers such action desirable. It must be construed that the word "desirable" is more appropriate than was "reasonable" under the old subsection.

A child 12 years or older will receive a copy of the report, unless the court is satisfied that the report in whole or in part could cause "emotional harm." This is the same test used to decide the matter of notice to a child under s. 39(4), closed or public hearings under s. 41(4), and the exclusion of media personnel under s. 41(7). Once again, the wording of the old Act – "injurious to the emotional health of the child" – is changed to "would cause emotional harm to the child."

In contrast to the predecessor Act, the distinguishing age has been increased in the new Act, from 10 to 12 years. Further, as noted above, the criteria for the court's decision are changed:

(1)   from "reasonable in the circumstances" to "desirable"; and
(2)   from injury to the child's "emotional health", to "emotional harm".

The Act stipulates that a child less than 12 years shall not receive a copy, but that the child's solicitor shall receive one (see s. 50(3)). While there is no *express* prohibition imposed upon child's counsel in such circumstances, not to provide the child with a copy, it would appear to be a constraint imposed upon counsel. Counsel,

(i)   wishing to give the child client a copy of the report; and
(ii)   believing it "desirable" that the child "receive a copy";

is at liberty to apply to the court to seek its sanction under s. 50(4) to the release of the report to the child client.

The Act gives such counsel, where the child does not receive the report, no guidance as to whether the contents in whole or in part may be disclosed to the child. Indeed, while the section addresses the matter of "disclosure" at s. 50(5), (where it seems to equate its meaning with that of "receive a copy"), that word is not used at s. 50(4). Can counsel *read* the report to the child under 12, (but not provide a copy) and escape the effect of the section? Or is the word "receive" to be given so broad a connotation that it is to cover any form of conveyance of the report or its content? It would seem that the prohibition against any delivey of the report to the child by counsel, (giving or reading), would most reasonably meet the intent of the section. In short, non-disclosure is designed to protect the child under 12, unless a court considers it otherwise "desirable". Should counsel, in direct contravention of the section, disclose the content or deliver the report to the child, there appear to be no sanctions in the Act. Such disclosure could constitute a breach of professional conduct and be contrary to obligations as an "officer of the court". However, significant considerations would flow from the rebuttal that the solicitor-client relationship might not have been meaningful or survived had full disclosure not been provided.

Where counsel does not disclose the content of the report to the child client, he or she is to rely upon the obligation to advocate what counsel believes the child's best interests to be.

S. 50(6): Report on Evidence

> (6) The report of an assessment ordered under subsection (1) is evidence and is part of the court record of the proceeding.

A very similar provision was in the *Child Welfare Act* at s. 29(4).

COMMENTARY:

Under this provision, the report becomes part of the court record once it is ordered by the court, received by the court, and the notice requirements of s. 50(3) are fulfilled. It becomes then, a statutory exception to the hearsay rule. Counsel should be on guard as to the implications of this provision and the need to consider a subpoena to compel the maker of the report to attend at court for examination on the report.

The distinction between court ordered and voluntary assessments should be kept in mind; this section refers only to the former.

S. 50(7): Inference From Refusal

> (7) The court may draw any inference it considers reasonable from a person's refusal to undergo an assessment ordered under subsection (1).

The equivalent subsection under the *Child Welfare Act* was s. 29(5).

COMMENTARY:

The drafters have retained the essential ingredient: that the court might draw any "inference" from a person's refusal to undergo assessment. They appear though to have widened the scope over which such inference might be applied, by the deletion of the words "relating to the placement of the child" found in s. 29(5) of the *Child Welfare Act*. As a result, a court might use such inferences in connection with other matters, including the issue of that person's access to a child in care.

S. 50(8): Inadmissibility of Report

> (8)   The report of an assessment ordered under subsection (1) is not admissible into evidence in any other proceeding except,
> (a)   an appeal in the proceeding under section 65;
> (b)   a proceeding under the *Coroners Act*; or
> (c)   a proceeding referred to in section 77 (recovery on child's behalf).
> without the consent of the person or persons assessed.

The equivalent provision in the *Child Welfare Act* was at s. 29(4).

COMMENTARY:

Section 50(8) bars the admission of the assessment report in other proceedings except:

(1)   One of the three specifically sanctioned proceedings as enumerated (a) through (c); or

(2)   with the consent of the person or persons assessed.

As a result, admission of such a report in a proceeding by way of judicial review, remains excluded.

SECTION 51. CONSENT ORDERS

This section includes a further checklist for the court on applications brought before it which are on the consent of the parties.

> s. 51   Where a child is brought before the court on consent as described in clause 37(2)(l), the court shall, before making an order under section 53 that would remove the child from the parent's care and custody,

(a)   ask whether,
  (i) the society has offered the parent and child ser-
       vices that would enable the child to remain with
       the parent, and
  (ii) the parent and, where the child is twelve years of
       age or older, the child has consulted independent
       legal counsel in connection with the consent; and
(b)   be satisfied that,
  (i) the parent and, where the child is twelve years of
       age or older, the child understands the nature and
       consequences of the consent,
  (ii) every consent is voluntary, and
  (iii) the parent and, where the child is twelve years of
       age or older, the child consents to the order being
       sought.

There was no equivalent section in the *Child Welfare Act*. (see below).

COMMENTARY:

For the most part this section is entirely new. The exception is s.
51(a)(i), which bears a partial resemblance to s. 30(5) of the *Child
Welfare Act*. That section directs that a court inquire into a society's
efforts to assist a child while the child was still outside the society's
care. (see discussion of s. 49(1), *supra*).

  In s. 51, the statute is essentially giving legislative effect to an
existing practice of judges of the Provincial Court (Family Division).
Where a consent matter has come before the court, the result of
which could be the removal of a child from the family setting,
whether temporarily (society wardship) or permanently (Crown
wardship), the court has consistently made inquiries to satisfy itself
that:

(a)   the parties have had the opportunity where appropriate to
      consult counsel and to have had the benefit of independent
      legal advice;
(b)   that the consent is voluntary and that the party giving it under-
      stands its nature and possible consequences;
(c)   that the child, where appropriate, given age considerations,
      consents.

  The evident intent is that this practice be applied uniformly and
consistently across the province. There will be two probable implications of such an extension:

(a)   the possibility that a child will have independent legal counsel,
      without regard for the criteria of s. 38(4) addressing the matter
      of legal representation for a child, unless the child is otherwise

able to satisfy a court of his or her understanding and consent to the proposed plan;

(b) that a child of 12 years or more must consent to the removal and that consent will have to be voluntary and properly understood and appreciated by the child.

It should be noted that the section does not imply that counsel *must* be engaged by a parent or child of 12 years and over. The court is only obliged to inquire. Will it mean automatic referral of a child for "independent legal representation"? Probably not; but practically, such referral would make sense. A court may be less likely to be satisfied on the criteria under s. 51(b) in a case where a parent or child has not had the benefit of independent legal advice.

The obligations upon a society are in s. 51(a)(i). While a court need only *ask* about such services in order to discharge its obligation, it is appropriate given "best interests" considerations (and in particular those considerations in ss. 37(3), (5), (7) and (11), and the principles in the opening declaration (see s. 1(b) and (c)), to conclude that a court will pay more than "lip service" to these stipulations and require satisfaction that removal of the child is the only course offering the "least restrictive and disruptive course of action . . .".

This section should be read concomitantly with s. 4, which deals with consents and participation in agreements.

In addition, having regard for the wide implication of s. 4, relative to a child, one must have regard for the provisions of s. 104 of the Act dealing with the child's right to be informed. In particular the opening words of the section are significant, "A child in care has a right to be informed, in language suitable for the child's level of understanding . . .".

SECTION 52. SOCIETY'S PLAN FOR CHILD

This section requires that the court, having decided that protection is necessary, consider a written plan, to be prepared by the society, giving details of its proposal for wardship or supervision of the child.

> **s. 52 The court shall, before making an order under section 53 or 61, obtain and consider a plan for the child's care prepared in writing by the society and including,**
>
> **(a) a description of the services to be provided to remedy the condition or situation on the basis of which the child was found to be in need of protection;**
>
> **(b) a statement of the criteria by which the society will determine when its wardship or supervision was no longer required;**

(c)   an estimate of the time required to achieve the purpose of the society's intervention;

(d)   where the society proposes to remove or has removed the child from a person's care,

(i)   an explanation of why the child cannot be adequately protected while in the person's care, and a description of any past efforts to do so, and

(ii)   a statement of what efforts, if any, are planned to maintain the child's contact with the person; and

(e)   where the society proposes to remove or has removed the child from a person's care permanently, a description of the arrangements made or being made for the child's long-term stable placement.

There was no equivalent section in the *Child Welfare Act:* See *Commentary* below.

COMMENTARY:

The section rests on the assumption that the court has already found a child to be in need of protection and is contemplating an intervention, which the court deems necessary to protect that child in the future. Any such intervention must take the form of an order made by the court under s. 53, or a status review order. The section places an obligation: on the society to prepare a plan in writing, and on the court to "obtain and consider" such a plan prior to making an order under either of the two ss. 53 or 61.

Section 52 is entirely new except for the provision at (d)(i), which bears a resemblance to s. 30(5) of the *Child Welfare Act.* Nevertheless, its effect is again, to a large extent, simply to codify into law a practice which has become fairly general across the province.

A question arises as to how this written plan is to be presented to the court. The section seems to leave it up to the court to decide how it will "obtain" the plan. It is noteworthy that there is no explicit statutory obligation to provide a copy of such written plan to any party or to the child's counsel prior to the hearing. Such party or counsel will have to continue to rely on the tools as provided by the Rules and pre-trial examination and on informal society disclosure practices. It does not have the safeguard of s. 50(3), where an assessor's report must be provided at least seven days before hearing.

In addition, the implications of s. 46(2) bear on the timing of admission of the plan. With the exception of matter addressed in s. 52(d)(i), it would appear that all the subsections pertain to disposition. Hence they would appear to be restricted from admission until after the protection finding had been made on the protection application. Only those types of evidence that contain elements relating to protection and disposition may be admissible, given the wording of s. 46(2) and placing particular emphasis on the use of the word "only".

The plan may fall into the category of a "business record" as contemplated by s. 35 of the *Evidence Act* R.S.O. 1980, c. 145. Were that the case, then on the appropriate notice being given to parties as to its admission, it could, under the terms of that section, be admitted into evidence. Otherwise, through its author (presumably, the primary caseworker or supervisor) in his or her examination in court, its admission could be made.

The specificity of such plan will have to await caselaw determination, particularly in respect of the service plan proposed. Will the court require detailed specifics as to the mechanics; the who, what, when, where and how? How onerous will the obligation become and may such plan return to haunt a children's aid society on a review?

On the other hand, if fairness and certainty to a child and parents are to be assured in the court-sanctioned delivery of services to a child and family, the court must have such particulars in writing from a society.

At s. 52(e) there is reference to "arrangements made or being made for the child's long-term stable placement." In cases of anticipated permanent removal from a person's care, this may be construed as seeking information as to adoptability in the case of Crown wardship applications.

Finally, a difference might be noted between s. 52(e) and s. 49(2), in the matter of protecting the identity of foster parents or those persons providing placement. Section 49(1)(b) requires that the court, in making an order, "shall give a statement of every plan for the child's care proposed to the court"; and s. 49(2) points out that this does not require the court to identify any person or place involved. No similar restriction pertaining to identification is included in s. 52(e), regarding long-term placement plans by the society. The purpose of not making identification would seem to be both to protect privacy and to provide for greater flexibility in any subsequent change to the statement under s. 49(1)(b).

The section has advantage to a children's aid society. While providing minimum standards, it directs a caseworker to set out the "roadmap" for the case. It may assist in prompting caseworkers to clarify their own thinking on the case. Expectations by a society, of parents, can be detailed. Indeed, an alert caseworker may wish to specify with particularity, the society's expectations of parents during a specified time frame. It should not be construed as unreasonable to have such attached to any plan.

Likewise, by virtue of the expectations of all persons being established in the plan, other parties would know where they stand.

The disadvantage to a society of such is, that it may give the intrusive judge the "open door" through which he or she can pass into case management decision-making analysis. A society may as a result, find itself on the horns of a dilemma: how much to disclose for the "curious judiciary" as against the extent to which specificity is in the client's interests.

The section is unclear as to whether it can include conditional terms, which if breached could permit a "triggering" in procedure and review by a court. Having regard for s. 60(8)(b), this is contemplated.

SECTION 53. ORDER WHERE CHILD IN NEED OF PROTECTION

This section requires the court to issue an order when it finds a child to be in need of protection. The section presents five possible dispositions, from which the court must choose one, having in mind the "best interests" of the child. In the subsections, several limitations and restrictions are placed on these orders.

S. 53(1): Optional Orders Upon a Protection Finding

(1)   Where the court finds that a child is in need of protection and is satisfied that intervention through a court order is necessary to protect the child in the future, the court shall make one of the following orders, in the child's best interests:
  1.   That the child be placed with or returned to a parent or another person, subject to the supervision of the society, for a specified period of at least three and not more than twelve months.
  2.   That the child be made a ward of the society and be placed in its care and custody for a specified period not exceeding twelve months.
  3.   That the child be made a ward of the Crown, until the wardship is terminated under section 61 or expires under subsection 67(1), and be placed in the care of the society.
  4.   That the child be made a ward of the society under paragraph 2 for a specified period and then be returned to a parent or another person under paragraph 1, for a period or periods not exceeding an aggregate of twelve months.

The equivalent provision of the *Child Welfare Act* was at s. 30(1).

COMMENTARY:

The subsection enumerates the remedies available to the court on a protection finding. It is to be noted that the court has no jurisdiction to use these remedies prior to a protection finding being made. In summary, the remedies included in subsection (1) provide that the child may be:

(1)   placed with or returned to parent or other person, with society supervision; for a period of three to 12 months;
(2)   made a ward of the society; maximum, 12 months;
(3)   made a ward of the Crown until this is terminated or expires as provided in the Act;
(4)   made a ward of the society, and later returned to parent or other person, under supervision; aggregate period: 12 months or less.

Minor changes from the old Act include the reduction of the minimum period in (1) above, from six to three months. One significant addition found in the new Act is the inclusion of remedy no. 4, society wardship followed by return to the parent or other person. This allows the court to combine society wardship and supervision orders without the necessity of a status review. In making such an order, the court will likely rely heavily on the proposed plan required of the society under s. 52.

A further observation pertains to the wording of option one compared to option four, which seems to imply a restriction on the range of persons to whose care a child may be committed under option four:

(a)   the child "be placed with or returned to a parent or another person . . ."
(b)   the child "be returned to a parent or another person . . ."

The difference in wording carries a strong suggestion that, whereas under (1) the court is free to place the child without restriction, under (4) the placement can be only with someone (parent or another person) in whose care the child has previously been. This must be done "under paragraph 1." – which would imply, "subject to society supervision, for a specified period of at least three and not more than twelve months." On the face of it, the reduction of the minimum time in option one from six months to three, is an accommodation to the introduction of option four.

CASE LAW: S. 53(1):

Re M.G.L.D. et al.; A.D. and R.D. v. Porcupine and Dist. C.A.S. (1984), 41 R.F.L. (2d) 176 (Ont. Div. Ct.).

Under s. 30(1)(3) a Crown wardship order cannot be made with conditions attached to it. Such conditions would be severable and of no effect on the jurisdiction of a court to make a Crown wardship order.

Re C.D. (1983), 36 R.F.L. (2d) 70 (Ont. Prov. Ct.).
Application by society to extend original 72-hour society wardship for an additional period of time on the basis that the newborn may require emergency medical treatment and blood transfusion, to which the biological parent had refused to consent. The court held that the infant continues to remain in need of protection given that the parent *may* refuse medical attention to the child that *may* be required. The court, in circumstances such as these, does not have to wait until treatment has been, in fact, refused. Society wardship was extended for 21 days.

D. v. C.A.S. of Kent County (1980), 18 R.F.L. (2d) 223 (Ont. Co. Ct.). See s. 37(2).

Re C.A.S. Metro. Toronto and P. (1979), 27 O.R. (2d) 55 (Prov. Ct.). The 24-month limitation period found in s. 25 and s. 37 applies to an order pursuant to s. 30(1) para. 2. Thus a child cannot be in the continuous care of a society for more than 24 months regardless of how the care by the society was established.

Re C. (1983), 20 A.C.W.S. (2d) 49 (Ont. Prov. Ct.).
Where a child is determined to be in need of protection the court must make one of the orders provided in s. 30. The society may not discontinue the application.

S. 53(2): Court to Inquire of Past Efforts to Assist Child

(2)   In determining which order to make under subsection (1), the court shall ask the parties what efforts the society or another agency or person made to assist the child before intervention under this Part.

A similar provision was contained in the *Child Welfare Act* at s. 30(5).

COMMENTARY:

Special prominence is given in these proceedings to the background of efforts made to assist the child prior to intervention. As seen above at s. 52(d)(i), the written plan prepared by the society must contain "a description of any past efforts to [protect the child adequately]". The current subsection specifically directs the court to ask the parties about such efforts. The force of the subsection has been strengthened in the new Act, which inquires of the parties "what efforts" rather than "whether any efforts have been made" as in the old Act. Thus subsection 53(2), like the five subsections which follow it, sets down conditions under which an order under subsection (1) can be made.

S. 53(3): Use of Removal Order Restricted

(3)   The court shall not make an order removing the child from the care of the person who had charge of him or her immediately before intervention under this Part unless the court is satisfied that less restrictive alternatives, including non-residential services and the assistance referred to in subsection (2),

(a)   have been attempted and have failed;

(b)   have been refused by the person having charge of the child; or

(c)   would be inadequate to protect the child.

There was no equivalent section in the *Child Welfare Act.*

COMMENTARY:

This subsection is entirely new. It picks up the thrust of s. 1(b) and (c) of the Declaration of Principles. Prior to making any order which would involve the removal of a child, the court must review all the available alternatives which might be "less restrictive", and must be satisfied that none of these could be successfully applied. A children's aid society will most often be the applicant seeking relief under s. 53(1). Hence, the obligation will rest on the society to offer evidence on (i) the available alternatives that have been attempted and how these have fared under s. 53(3)(a) and (b), or (ii) why such alternatives would be inadequate. Where the use of "less restrictive" alternatives is simply not appropriate (e.g. physical or sexual child abuse where "abuser parent"denies the allegations) and the child is at risk, the society will rely on part (c).

S. 53(4): Community Placement to be Considered

(4)   Where the court decides that it is necessary to remove the child from the care of the person who had charge of him or her immediately before intervention under this Part, the court shall, before making an order for society or Crown wardship under paragraph 2 or 3 of subsection (1), consider whether it is possible to place the child with a relative, neighbour or other member of the child's community or extended family under paragraph 1 of subsection (1) with the consent of the relative or other person.

This subsection has no counterpart in the *Child Welfare Act.*

COMMENTARY:

As in the foregoing subsection, this one applies before any order can be made which would involve the removal of a child. Again, it takes its thrust from the Declaration of Principles in s. 1, especially clauses (c), (d) and (e). It also reflects the "best interests" test criteria at s. 37(3), paragraphs 5 and 7, relating to the importance in the child's development, of positive and continuous family ties.

Under this subsection, the court is required to "consider" certain options before any such removal order is made, namely the possibility of placement with:

(a)   a relative;
(b)   a neighbour;
(c)   another member of the child's community or extended family (see definition s. 37(1)(c)).

Such person must, of course, consent to the placement.

The Act gives no express direction concerning the party on whom the obligation to make out the matter of family or community placement lies. It probably is upon the applicant society. If it is, however, the subsection fails to take into account the obstacles facing the society in getting information from family or relative sources. This is because of the confidentiality constraints imposed on service providers as to the disclosure of information about children and parents. These constraints are found in Part VIII of the Act. In short, given confidentiality rules, the society will be unable (without information releases or written consents from the parents and sometimes the child) to disclose to alternative family, relative or community placements the circumstances about which inquiries are being made as to *their* availability for supplying placement for a child.

There is no direction given concerning the *extent* to which, or the *manner* in which the court is to "consider" these placement options. Must the court record reflect the considerations? Is simply a statement to the effect that these options have been considered sufficient?

The wording of the subsection is broad. It appears to allow significant leeway on the number of persons available for consideration. A parent's counsel will undoubtedly rely on relief under subsection (4), to keep a child in the community and close to a parent. However, in circumstances of substantiated child abuse, the court will undoubtedly consider such alternative placements carefully, before ordering placement.

S. 53(5): Further Restriction in Case of Indian or Native Person

(5)   Where the child referred to in subsection (4) is an Indian or a

native person, unless there is a substantial reason for placing
the child elsewhere, the court shall place the child with,

(a)   a member of the child's extended family;

(b)   a member of the child's band or native community; or

(c)   another Indian or native family.

There was no equivalent subsection in the *Child Welfare Act*.

COMMENTARY:

This subsection is a special application of subsection (4), to the case
where the child is an Indian or a native person. The legislation
recognizes the unique cultural differences of the Indian or native
person. The Indian band or native community's role in the life of one
of its own children is distinctive. Therefore a court's power is restricted in the matter of placement of such child. A court determining
the need to remove an Indian or native child from the parent is
directed to select one of three alternative placements, set out in (a)
through (c). Only where "substantial reason" exists in favour of some
other alternative may a court direct a placement other than those
listed above. It would appear that this need not require establishing
reasons "against" placement in one of the three listed alternatives,
but only that, on balance, the reasons for placing the child elsewhere
are stronger.

The scope of "substantial reason" will have to await caselaw
determination. Where no Indian or native placement is available, the
subsection will have insignificant impact. However, where a placement is available, how will it bear upon the definition of "substantial
reason", where on a competing scale there are such facts as:

(a)   a mixed marriage, and the non-Indian or non-native "parent" is
        seeking child's placement with him or her;

(b)   that the Indian or native community does not wish the child
        placed;

(c)   the child's medical condition dictates placement in or near a
        metropolitan centre with special medical equipment;

(d)   the child has special education needs, for which the Indian or
        native placement has not the facilities.

Which consideration will override – the need for Indian or native
community placement and the device to maintain cultural continuity,
or serving the child's other needs and interests? The Declaration of
Principles itself at s. 1(f) states that its intent must be subject to the
proviso of "wherever possible".

The court will consider the suitability of placement options (a)
through (c) on the representation of the representative of the child's
band or native community under s. 39(1)(4).

S. 53(6): Restriction on any Order for Crown Wardship

(6)   The court shall not make an order for Crown wardship under paragraph 3 of subsection (1) unless the court is satisfied that the circumstances justifying the order are unlikely to change within a reasonably foreseeable time not exceeding twenty-four months so that the child can be returned to the care of the person who had charge of him or her immediately before intervention under this Part.

There was no equivalent section in the *Child Welfare Act*.

COMMENTARY:

Like the foregoing subsections, this is a restriction imposed on an order by the court. A court shall not contemplate an order for Crown wardship unless the circumstances upon which such order would be made, are unlikely to change within the ensuing 24 months. This is a strong restriction on the use of an order for Crown wardship. "Unlikely to change" would seem to carry the same force as "likely *not* to change". In that case, what must be demonstrated is that there is *positive* reason to expect that there will be *no* change. This clearly carries a heavier onus than does demonstrating that there is *no* reason to expect *some* change. Thus the justification for an order for Crown wardship appears to have been made heavy indeed. Obviously, if any such change is anticipated or is seen as a probability, a court is *obliged* to consider the lesser remedy of society wardship (see s. 53(1) and (2)).

The subsection emphasizes what is the widely understood practice. Crown wardship being an order with finality (subject only to limited review conditions under s. 60), which may result in adoption placement, such a disposition should be made only where every reasonable prospect is that the condition which has to be remedied is a permanent one. This, of course, enhances the importance of the society's written plan to a court and particularly s. 52(a) through (c). Furthermore, it underscores the significance of the court's inquiries at s. 53(2) and (3).

S. 53(7): Notice-restriction on Wardship Orders

(7)   When the court has dispensed with notice to a person under subsection 39(7), the court shall not make an order for Crown wardship under paragraph 3 of subsection (1), or an order for society wardship under paragraph 2 of subsection (1) for a period exceeding thirty days, until a further hearing under subsection 43(1) has been held upon notice to that person.

There was no equivalent subsection in the *Child Welfare Act*.

COMMENTARY:

Subsection 39(7) entitles a court to dispense with notice to a person where the time required might "endanger the child's health or safety." The court might use this where a show cause hearing is required under s. 42.

   The current subsection provides, however, that such an order would bar the court from making an order of society or Crown wardship without notification to that person, by personal or substituted service. Where notice has not been effected, the court may make no order having an effect for more than a 30-day period. The section underscores the serious import of a society or Crown wardship order. It has no application to supervision dispositions.

S. 53(8): Terms and Conditions of Supervision Order

    (8)   Where the court makes a supervision order under paragraph 1 of subsection (1), the court may impose reasonable terms and conditions relating to the child's care and supervision on,

    (a)   the person with whom the child is placed or to whom the child is returned;

    (b)   the supervising society;

    (c)   the child; and

    (d)   any other person who participated in the hearing.

The equivalent provision in the *Child Welfare Act* was at s. 30(4).

COMMENTARY:

With minor modifications, this is identical to its predecessor provision. The court is given the authority, in making a supervision order, to impose terms and conditions upon persons described in (a) through (d). The term "method of supervision" found in the old Act has been replaced with "care and supervision". This may be considered a broadening of the court's scope and latitude. Conditions must relate to the "care and supervision" of the child; hence conditions that deal with parents and their conduct are beyond the court's jurisdiction.

S. 53(9): Where No Court Order is Necessary

    (9)   Where the court finds that a child is in need of protection but is not satisfied that a court order is necessary to protect the child in the future, the court shall order that the child remain

with or be returned to the person who had charge of the child immediately before intervention under this Part.

There was no equivalent provision in the *Child Welfare Act.*

COMMENTARY:

Section 30 of the old law imposed a duty upon a court where it found a child to be "in need of protection." That duty was to select one of the three options as an order – supervision, society or Crown wardship.

The current subsection provides an option not available under the *Child Welfare Act.* It allows a court, even in the face of a protection finding, not to make one of the orders prescribed earlier in the section. The court must be satisfied that such an order is not necessary to protect the child in the future. In this case the court may order the child returned to the person who had charge, immediately before, with no restriction. Subsection (9) in effect provides a fifth option for the court in the case of a protection finding.

The "need for protection" in such case would unquestionably have to be minor, technical or isolated. The court would have to be satisfied that the possibility of recurrence is so marginal that the net effect of court or society interference would be adverse rather than positive.

A further question remains. Does the protection finding which is subsumed in s. 53, actually find itself incorporated into the order? If protection is so found, is it a continuing condition? The section is of no assistance on this point. However, the practical consequence is that the finding leads to disposition, after which the protection finding itself appears to have no further significance.

The order provided for in subsection (9) does not constitute an order for status review purposes because there is no supervision, society or Crown wardship disposition (s. 60(1)). It is simply a return without condition. The court has no authority to order any other assistance for the child. This option will be attractive to counsel for parents given that it avoids a status review hearing at any time in the future. The continuing stigma often associated with a "protection" finding may also be diminished.

SECTION 54. ACCESS

This section sets the conditions under which a court may issue access orders, either when making an order under Part III or upon an application. The section is here treated in its entirety.

S. 54(1): Access Order

(1)   The court may, in the child's best interests,

(a)   when making an order under this Part; or

(b)   upon an application under subsection (2),

make, vary or terminate an order respecting a person's access to the child or the child's access to a person, and may impose such terms and conditions on the order as the court considers appropriate.

S. 54(2): Who May Apply

(2)   Where the child is in a society's care and custody or supervision,

(a)   the child;

(b)   any other person, including, where the child is an Indian or a native person, a representative chosen by the child's band or native community; or

(c)   the society.

may apply to the court at any time for an order under subsection (1).

S. 54(3) and (4): Notice

(3)   An applicant referred to in clause (2)(b) shall give notice of the application to the society.

(4)   A society making or receiving an application under subsection (2) shall give notice of the application to,

(a)   the child, subject to subsections 39(4) and (5) (notice to child);

(b)   the child's parent;

(c)   the person caring for the child at the time of the application; and

(d)   where the child is an Indian or a native person, a representative chosen by the child's band or native community.

S. 54(5): Child Over Sixteen

(5)   No order respecting access to a person sixteen years of age or more shall be made under subsection (1) without the person's consent.

S. 54(6): Six Month Period

(6)   No application shall be made under subsection (2) by a person other than a society within six months of,

(a)   the making of an order under section 53;

(b)   the disposition of a previous application by the same person under subsection (2);

    (b)   the disposition of an application under section 60 (review); or

    (d)   the final disposition or abandonment of an appeal from an order referred to in clause (a), (b) or (c),

whichever is later.

S. 54(7): No Application Where Child Placed for Adoption

  (7)   No person or society shall make an application under subsection (2) where the child,

    (a)   is a Crown ward;

    (b)   has been placed in a person's home by the society or by a Director for the purpose of adoption under Part VII (Adoption); and

    (c)   still resides in that person's home.

The equivalent provision in the *Child Welfare Act* was at s. 35.

COMMENTARY:

Under this section, the court may make, vary or terminate an order governing the right of access to a child who is in a society's care and custody or under its supervision. The court may act on its own or on an application (s. 54(1)(a)). The criterion to be applied is that of the child's best interests. There is virtually no restriction on who may apply to the court for such an order, including the child and the society itself. However, any person applying for an access order, with the exception of the child and the society, must so notify the society, which in turn must notify the persons listed in subsection (4). Subsection (6) restricts the timing of such applications relative to orders under s. 53 and previous applications or appeals. However, a society can bring an application at any time; and seek to establish the conditions under which applications are not permitted.

    The scope of those who may apply for access has been widened in the new Act by the addition of "any other person" and by reference to Indian and native community representation. The greater ambit allows persons to apply who may never have had care of the child; for example, grandparents. The inclusion of Indian or band representative acknowledges the special status of native peoples and the importance of maintaining a child's cultural heritage.

SECTION 55. ACCESS

This section governs, in cases where a child has been removed from the person who had charge immediately previously, access by that person. Special problems are covered in the case where the child is a Crown ward.

S. 55(1). Access: Where Child Removed from Person in Charge

(1)   Where an order is made under paragraph 1 or 2 of subsection 53(1) removing a child from the person who had charge of the child immediately before intervention under this Part, the court shall make an order for access by the person unless the court is satisfied that continued contact with him or her would not be in the child's best interests.

S. 55(2): Crown Ward

(2)   Where a child is made a Crown ward under paragraph 3 of subsection 53(1), the court shall not make an order for access by the person who had charge of the child immediately before intervention under this Part unless the court is satisfied that,

(a)   permanent placement in a family setting has not been planned or is not possible, and the person's access will not impair the child's future opportunities for such placement;

(b)   the child is at least twelve years of age and wishes to maintain contact with the person;

(c)   the child has been or will be placed with a person who does not wish to adopt the child; or

(d)   some other special circumstance justifies making an order for access.

S. 55(3): Termination of Access to Crown Ward

(3)   The court shall not terminate an order for access to a Crown ward unless the court is satisfied that the circumstances that justified the making of the order under subsection (2) no longer exist.

For equivalent provisions in the *Child Welfare Act*, see Commentary.

COMMENTARY:

There was no *Child Welfare Act* equivalent to s. 55(1). The subsection obligates a court, when removing a child from the person who had charge of the child, to make an order for access by such person. The court may decline to make such an order if satisfied that it is contrary to the child's best interest. Such a finding by a court would have to be based on the evidence and the "best interests" test. This is really only a codification of existing practice. Such a provision has no application on an interim proceeding before the protection finding is made.

Subsection 55(2) concerns access by the person having charge of the child before intervention, where the child has been made a Crown ward. Here, access is not to be permitted *except* on the basis of the criteria specified (a) through (d). Given the subsection's wording, the onus to satisfy the court that the criteria are fulfilled, appears to fall upon the person seeking such access. However, given the formulation of s. 55(2)(a), the society's plan at s. 52 and in particular the information at s. 52(e) will be critical to a court assessing access.

The child's position concerning access in the operation of this section is significant. The child of at least 12 years may by his or her own expressed position, bring about access where it would otherwise not be directed. (See s. 55(2)(b)).

The "catch-all" of s. 55(2)(d) remains unclear, since it uses the wider criterion of "special circumstance"; it will have to await case-law determination for more certainty.

Once an order for access to a Crown ward is in place under s. 55(2), it may only be terminated under s. 55(3) upon a court's being satisfied that the conditions of s. 55(2)(a) through (d), upon which the order was made, no longer exist. Such a development, resulting in prohibition of access, could be significant to a society, since it would clear the society's path where the society plans for the adoption of the child, an irreversible step. The onus will be upon the party seeking the relief. A court will undoubtedly sense the objective of a society on such an application and impose a rather high standard of proof, in order to meet the point of satisfaction dictated by the section.

CASE LAW: S. 55:

L.G. and M.G. (1983), 30 R.F.L. (2d) 103 (Ont. Prov. Ct.).
Terms of access provided in a decree *nisi* of Divorce do not inhibit the jurisdiction of a Provincial Court (Family Division) Judge under s. 35 of the *Child Welfare Act* from considering access in favour of a non-custodial parent. The court adopted the dicta in *Re C.C.A.S. of Metro. Toronto*, [1972] 2 O.R. 598, 7 R.F.L. 190 (*sub nom. R. Caron; C.C.A.S. of Metro. Toronto v. Chambers*) 26 D.L.R. (3d) 266 (H. C.J.). Furthermore the court asserted that "where a child is before the court pursuant to a child protection legislation, there is no jurisdiction to grant access to that child pursuant to any other legislation," adopting the dicta in *Re Fortowsky and Essex R.C. C.A.S.*, [1960] O.W.N. 235, 23 D.L.R. (2d) 569 (C.A.), and *Cox v. Metro. Toronto C.A.S.* (1979), 23 O.R. (2d) 351, 8 R.F.L. (2d) 391 (Prov. Ct.).

SECTION 56. PAYMENT ORDERS

This section provides for payments by parents to the society, to help support children who are in the society's care or supervision. The criteria for setting such payments, conditions for variation and expiry, and enforcement of payment, are included.

S. 56(1): Order for Payment by a Parent

(1) Where the court places a child in the care of,
   (a) a society; or
   (b) a person other than the child's parent, subject to a society's supervision,
   the court may order a parent or a parent's estate to pay the society a specified amount at specified intervals for each day the child is in the society's care or supervision.

S. 56(2): Criteria

(2) In making an order under subsection (1), the court shall consider those of the following circumstances of the case that the court considers relevant:
   1. The assets and means of the child and of the parent or the parent's estate.
   2. The child's capacity to provide for his or her own support.
   3. The capacity of the parent or the parent's estate to provide support.
   4. The child's and the parent's age and physical and mental health.
   5. The child's mental, emotional and physical needs.
   6. Any legal obligation of the parent or the parent's estate to provide support for another person.
   7. The child's aptitude for and reasonable prospects of obtaining an education.
   8. Any legal right of the child to support from another source, other than out of public moneys.

S. 56(3): Order Ends at Eighteen

(3) No order made under subsection (1) shall extend beyond the day on which the child attains the age of eighteen years.

S. 56(4): Power to Vary

(4) The court may vary, suspend or terminate an order made under subsection (1) where the court is satisfied that the circumstances of the child or parent have changed.

S. 56(5): Collection by Municipality

(5)   The council of a municipality may enter into an agreement with the board of directors of a society providing for the collection by the municipality, on the society's behalf, of the amounts ordered to be paid by a parent under subsection (1).

S. 56(6): Enforcement

(6)   An order made against a parent under subsection (1) may be enforced under sections 27 to 32 of the *Family Law Reform Act* as if it were an order for support.

The equivalent provision of the *Child Welfare Act* was at s. 31.

COMMENTARY:

With minor modifications the provisions of s. 56 are identical to those of the *Child Welfare Act.* Where a court directs that a child is to be:

(1)   a society ward (see s. 53(1) and (2));
      or
(b)   under society supervision in care of a person other than the child's parent,

a court may direct that the parent or the parent's estate pay what is, in effect, support for the child's care. Such support is paid to the society under whose care or supervision the child is placed. The payor must fall within the definition of "parent" as at s. 37(1)(d).

The court is directed to "consider", from a list of criteria, those which the court "considers" relevant. The list is contained in s. 56(2) paragraphs 1 through 8, and essentially includes:

(a)   the child's financial need (s. 56(2) paras. 4., 5., 7.);
(b)   the child's own capabilities of contributing to his or her own support (s. 56(2) paras. 1., 2., and 8.);
(c)   the ability of the parent or the estate to pay (s. 56(2) paras. 1., 3., 4., and 6.);

The test is virtually identical to the provisions for determining child support under s. 33(9) of the *Family Law Act,* S.O. 1986, c. 4.

A court is to take into account the right of the child to support from any other source other than public monies (see s. 56(2)8.). A support obligation cannot extend past the child's 18th birthday (s. 56(3)).

A court may change, suspend or terminate any order based on the "change of circumstances" test of either parent or child. It is noteworthy that the provisions of s. 56(4) for variation of payment do not adopt the identical test found at s. 37 in the *Family Law Act, 1986* S.O. 1986, c. 4, that the change must be "material" in order to warrant a variation.

Some questions remain to be decided. The provision does not expressly indicate who may apply for variation. Can it include a child, in addition to the society (facing an increased support obligation), and a parent (whose income capability perhaps has diminished)?

Collection under a payment order is directed by s. 56(5) and (6). Apart from agreements between a society and a municipality for collection, the society has all the remedies that a payee spouse would have as against the defaulting payor under the *Support and Custody Orders Enforcement Act, 1985,* S.O. 1985, c. 6 and *Family Law Act, 1986,* S.O. 1986, c. 4.

SECTION 57. SOCIETY AND CROWN WARDSHIP

This section establishes the criteria to be considered in choosing or changing a residential placement by a society, for a child who is a society or a Crown ward. The major responsibilities of the society to the child, and the rights of the child and parents (including foster parents) are also established.

S. 57

(1) This section applies where a child is made a society or Crown ward under paragrah 2 or 3 of subsection 53(1).
(2) The society having care of a child shall choose a residential placement for the child that,
   (a) represents the least restrictive alternative for the child;
   (b) where possible, respects the religious faith, if any, in which the child is being raised;
   (c) where possible, respects the child's linguistic and cultural heritage;
   (d) where the child is an Indian or a native person, is with a member of the child's extended family, a member of the child's band or native community or another Indian or native family, if possible; and
   (e) takes into account the child's wishes if they can be reasonably ascertained, and the wishes of any parent who is entitled to access to the child.
(3) The society having care of a child shall ensure that the child receives an education that corresponds to his or her aptitudes and abilities.
(4) The society having care of a child shall not place the child

outside Ontario or permit a person to remove the child from Ontario permanently unless a Director is satisfied that extraordinary circumstances justify the placement or removal.

(5) The society having care of a child shall ensure that,
   (a) the child is afforded all the rights referred to in Part V (Rights of Children); and
   (b) the wishes of any parent who is entitled to access to the child and, where the child is a Crown ward, of any foster parent with whom the child has lived continuously for two years are taken into account in the society's major decisions concerning the child.

(6) The society having care of a child may remove the child from a foster home or other residential placement where, in the opinion of a Director or local director, it is in the child's best interests to do so.

(7) Where a child is a Crown ward and has lived with a foster parent continuously for two years, the society shall not remove the child under subsection (6) without first giving the foster parent ten days notice of the proposed removal and of his or her right to a review under section 64.

(8) Where a foster parent requests a review under section 64 within ten days of receiving a notice under subsection (7), the society shall not remove the child until the review and any further review by a Director have been completed and unless the society's board of directors or the Director, as the case may be, recommend that the child be removed.

(9) Subsections (7) and (8) do not apply where, in the opinion of a Director or local director, there would be a substantial risk to the child's health or safety during the time necessary for notice to the foster parent and a review under section 64.

(10) Sections 34, 35 and 36 (review by Residential Placement Advisory Committee, further review by Children's Services Review Board) of Part II (Voluntary Access to Services) apply to a residential placement made by a society.

The similar provisions in the *Child Welfare Act* were found throughout ss. 40 and 45.

COMMENTARY:

Specifically, the *Child Welfare Act* covered the obligations of the society to a child within its care under an order of society or Crown wardship, in the matters of:

(1) placement (ss. 40(2), 45(1) and (2));
(2) education and training (s. 45(1)).
   In addition it extended to foster parents the opportunity to adopt a child in their care prior to any other adoption placement being effected (s. 45(3)).

The new law, on the other hand, sets out in considerably more detail, the obligations of the society and the rights of the *child*, the *parent* and the *foster parents*, especially as they pertain to initial placement, changes of placement and the child's education. Let us look at these rights in turn.

1. The Child:

In choosing a residential placement (as defined at s. 3(1) 25.), for a society or Crown ward, a society must take into account the factors itemized at s. 57(2)(a) through (e). The placement must represent the "least restrictive alternative for the child", thus applying the principle enshrined in the Declaration at s. 1(c). Likewise, changes in the residential placement must reflect the "best interests of the child" as seen by a Director or local director (see s. 57(6)).

Choice of a residential placement must "respect, where possible" the child's religious faith, and linguistic and cultural heritage. Further, the child's wishes (where ascertainable) are factors which a society must take into account. These provisions are new. The threads of the Declaration of Principles at s. 1(e) can be clearly seen.

The provisions of s. 57(2)(d) reflect the special treatment to be afforded a child of Indian or native background. A society, when dealing with either a society or a Crown ward, must consider a placement which will result in minimum disruption and the greatest continuity of this cultural tie.

Under s. 57(4), placement must be in Ontario unless the Director determines otherwise. Such a decision would require "extraordinary circumstances." While the Act provides no definition of such circumstances, the meaning probably relates to the exceptional case where specialized medical, psychological or psychiatric resources, or family, cultural, ethnic or religious considerations are taken into account to meet a child's unique needs.

The society, as under the *Child Welfare Act*, has the obligation to provide the education best suited to the child's "aptitudes and abilities." The "good parent" standard found in the *Child Welfare Act*, s. 45(1), has been replaced with a more objective standard in s. 57(3).

The society's care of a child must in addition, ensure that the rights of the child afforded by the provisions of Part V are protected.

2. The Parent:

The rights of parents as set forth at s. 57(2)(e), and (5)(b), are new. Parents entitled to access are to have their wishes taken into account on placement determinations (see s. 57(2)(e)). In addition, their wishes are to be taken into account in the society's "major decisions concerning the child" (see s. 57(5)(b)). Though the scope of such decisions is not expressly defined, they probably encompass matters of a medical, educational or religious nature, as well as decisions pertaining to the child's placement.

Conferring such rights on parents seems amply justified in both types of wardship. Where the child is the subject of a society wardship order, the premise upon which the order is made is that the child will return to the parent. During such wardship a parent should play an important role in the child's development – if not in the day-to-day care, then at least in the expression of ideas as to care.

Where the child is a Crown ward, if a parent has access entitlement, there must have been a judicial determination of the need for such access (see s. 55(2)). This being the case, access should be meaningful and confer upon an access parent opportunity for expression of thought and ideas about the child's best interest.

3. *The Foster Parent:*

The foster parents had a single right under s. 45(3) of the *Child Welfare Act:* the right to make an application to adopt a Crown ward who had been in their care, and whom the local director had decided to place for adoption.

The new provisions expand the rights of foster parents in whose care a child has been for two years. These are found in s. 57(5)(b), (7) and (8). The foster parents' right to have input into "major decisions" concerning the child are the same as for parents with access, already seen at s. 57(5)(b).

In addition under s. 57(7), where a child has been in a foster placement for two years, any removal of the child must be:

(1)   on ten days' notice to the foster parents, of the proposed removal;
(2)   after permitting the foster parents the opportunity to exercise their rights to a review under s. 64.

This right to notice and review does not apply in a case where, to discharge the terms of notice and review under s. 57(7) and (8), would expose a child to "substantial risk" to health or safety. (See s. 57(9)). In short, if the foster placement itself exposes the child to such risk, the society may move expeditiously to protect the child. However, the foster parents would still retain their rights for review under s. 64. In considering a change in foster placement, a Director shall take into account the criteria set out at s. 73(2).

Finally, where foster parent placement is not selected, but instead the child is provided with a residential service, then the review procedures of ss. 34, 35 and 36 of Part II are incorporated. This is achieved by s. 57(10).

SECTION 58. SOCIETY WARD: MEDICAL CONSENT AND OTHER CONSENTS

This section refers to a child who is a society ward, and sets out the respective rights of the society and the child's parent in consenting to, and authorizing, medical treatment for the child. Further, the parent's right in marriage consent is reaffirmed.

S. 58(1): Society Ward: Consent to Medical Treatment

Where a child is made a society ward under paragraph 2 of subsection 53(1), the society may consent to and authorize medical treatment for the child where a parent's consent would otherwise be required, unless the court orders that the parent shall retain any right that he or she may have to give or refuse consent to medical treatment for the child.

S. 58(2): Consent

(2) The court shall not make an order under subsection (1) where failure to consent to necessary medical treatment was a ground for finding that the child was in need of protection.

S. 58(3): Court Order

(3) Where a parent referred to in an order made under subsection (1) refuses or is unavailable or unable to consent to medical treatment for the child and the court is satisfied that the treatment would be in the child's best interests, the court may authorize the society to consent to the treatment.

S. 58(4): Consent to Child's Marriage

(4) Where a child is made a society ward under paragraph 2 of subsection 53(1), the child's parent retains any right that he or she may have under the *Marriage Act* to give or refuse consent to the child's marriage.

There was no equivalent provision in the *Child Welfare Act*.

COMMENTARY:

The purpose of s. 58 is to make clear the rights reserved to the parent of a society ward, primarily in the matter of medical treatment. Under subsection (1), a society has authority to provide consent and authorize such treatment when required. A court, however, may by order reserve that right to a parent.

This position reflects the principles set down at s. 1(b). In addition, it recognizes that despite a "protection finding", certain situations require the input of parents. "Protection" may result from isolated circumstances, so that, while ordering a temporary wardship, a court may not wish to otherwise strip parents of rights which bear upon the interests of their child. To illustrate, "protection" based on s. 37(2)(e) would be a case contemplated by this provision.

The provisions of s. 58(1), however, are tempered by the restriction imposed by s. 58(2). Where the situation described in that section exists (most likely on a protection finding under s. 37(2)(e), (f), (g) and (h)), the court may not exercise its discretion in s. 58(1).

Where an order under s. 58(1) reserves for a parent the right to consent, and the parent later refuses to exercise that consent, resulting in prejudice to the child's best interests, the court may revoke, vary or suspend its order. However, a society is obliged to demonstrate the ingredients of s. 58(3) and obtain the order, vesting it with such power before it can give the consent. Emergency circumstances could cause severe detriment to a child who requires urgent medical relief.

The final reservation of right to the parent of a society ward appears at s. 58(4). It is without reservation or qualification. The parent retains the right to give or refuse a consent to the child's marriage under s. 5(2) of the *Marriage Act* R.S.O. 1980, c. 256.

SECTION 59. SOCIETY AND CROWN WARDS: RIGHTS OF SOCIETY

This section confers upon the society, in the case of society and Crown wards, the rights and responsibilities of a parent for the purpose of the child's care.

S. 59(1): Crown Custodian of Crown Wards

(1)   Where a child is made a Crown ward under paragraph 3 of subsection 53(1), the Crown has the rights and responsibilities of a parent for the purpose of the child's care, custody and control and has the right to give or refuse consent to medical treatment for the child where a parent's consent would otherwise be required, and the Crown's powers, duties and obligations in respect of the child, except those assigned to a Director by this Act or the regulations, shall be exercised and performed by the society caring for the child.

S. 59(2): Society Custodian of Society Wards

(2)   Where a child is made a society ward under paragraph 2 of

> subsection 53(1), the society has the rights and the respon-
> sibilities of a parent for the purpose of the child's care,
> custody and control.

The equivalent provision of the *Child Welfare Act* was at ss. 40(1) and 41.

COMMENTARY:

The provisions of s. 59 set out on a general level the rights of a society for any Crown or society ward in its care. Like its predecessor the new Act directs that the "Crown" (in fact a society into whose charge a Crown ward has been placed) has the "rights and responsibilities" of a parent. This bundle of rights covers the wide range of the child's care, custody and control, including the right to "give or refuse" a consent to medical treatment. No rights are reserved to parents, as was done in the case of society wards under s. 58. The discharge of the Crown's rights in the case of Crown wards is generally under the authority of the society into whose care the Crown ward is placed. This is subject to the specific statutory or regulatory authority reserved to the Director as, for example, in ss. 62 and 73.

The provisions of s. 59(2) are the counterpart of s. 41 of the *Child Welfare Act.* With minor modification (most notably the deletion of "legal guardian" and in its place "parent") the society continues to have the right to deal as a parent with a society ward for purposes of "care, custody and control." This provision is restricted insofar as certain rights have been reserved to a parent at s. 58.

CASE LAW: S. 59:

Re A. and C.A.S. Metro. Toronto (1982), 141 D.L.R. (3d) 111 (Ont. Prov. Ct.).
Where a child has been apprehended and placed in the care of a society during a period of adjournment, that society has the authority to consent to emergency medical treatment of the child and non-emergency medical treatment.

Sections 60 to 64. REVIEW PROCEDURES

These sections establish routes for review, including review by the court, the Director, a judge appointed by the Minister and by the society.

S. 60(1): Application for Status Review

(1)   This section applies where a child is the subject of an order

for society supervision, society wardship or Crown wardship under subsection 53(1).

There was no similar provision in the *Child Welfare Act.*

COMMENTARY:

This section of the legislation is new. It establishes that an order of supervision, society or Crown wardship may be the subject of review.

S. 60(2): Society to Seek Status Review

(2)   The society having care, custody or supervision of a child,
   (a)   may apply to the court at any time, subject to subsection (9);
   (b)   where the order is for society supervision or society wardship, shall apply to the court before the expiry of the order, except under subsection 67(1) (age of eighteen); and
   (c)   where the society has removed the child from the care of a person with whom the child was placed under an order for society supervision, shall apply to the court within five days of the child's removal.
   for review of the child's status.

The equivalent provisions in the *Child Welfare Act* are s. 32(1), (2), s. 37(1) and s. 38(2).

COMMENTARY:

Under s. 60(2) a society can apply at any time to review a:

   (i) supervision order;
   (ii) society wardship order;
   (iii) Crown wardship order, except where the child,
      (a)   has been placed for adoption; and
      (b)   remains in that adoption placement.

Review of Supervision Orders: Under the *Child Welfare Act* s. 32(1), the society was under an obligation to apply to review the supervision order prior to its expiry. This obligation continues in s. 60(2)(b).

Review of Society Wardship Orders: Under the *Child Welfare Act* s. 37(1), the society was required to apply to review such an order before its expiry. This duty is continued under s. 60(2)(b).

Review of Crown Wardship Orders: Under the *Child Welfare Act* s. 38(2), the society could apply at any time to review an order of Crown wardship. Under s. 60(2)(a), taken in combination with s. 60(9) (see below), a society may *not* apply to review an order of Crown wardship where:

(a)   the child is a Crown ward; and
(b)   the child has been placed in a home for adoption; and
(c)   the child still resides in that home.

Section 60(2)(b) requires the society to apply to review supervision and society wardship orders before their expiry, unless the child reaches the age of 18 years or marries, in which case the society is not required to bring a review application. Where a child has been removed from a person's care, with whom he or she was placed under a supervision order, the society is required, under s. 60(2)(c), to apply for a status review within five days of the child's removal. This is similar to s. 32(2) of the *Child Welfare Act,* with the exception that under the older legislation, the application was to be made "as soon as is practicable, and within five days of removing a child . . .". Presumably this was intended to get the matter before the court in fewer than five days if possible.

CASE LAW: S. 60(2):

Caldwell v. C.A.S.Metro. Toronto (1976), 27 R.F.L. 259 (Ont. Prov. Ct.). Where a court is called upon to review a previous order, there having been a protection finding made, it is not obliged to consider a new protection finding. The test on such a review is the "best interests" of the child. The court applied *Petty v. Director of Child Welfare for Alberta* (1967), 59 W.W.R. 248, 61 D.L.R. (2d) 524 (Alta. C.A.), and *C.A.S. of Winnipeg v. Frohnen* (1975), 17 R.F.L. 47 (Man. C.A.) and stated, at p. 263 ". . . that once a finding is made under s. 20 of that Act that a child is a child in need of protection, it is then not necessary to make that finding again but the issue under s. 27(5) is really one of what is in the interest of the welfare of the child and only that."

C.A.S. Ottawa – Carleton v. D.J.L. and L.J.T.L. (1980), 15 R.F.L. (2d) 102 (Ont. Prov. Ct.).
On application for Crown wardship by way of a status review under s. 32(1) of a supervision order the court determined that the onus of proof was imposed upon the applicant society and that its standard was "upon a preponderance of the evidence." In this regard the court adopted the dicta in *Caldwell v. C.A.S. of Metro. Toronto* (1976), 27 R.F.L. 259 (Ont. Prov. Ct.). The court also considered on a status review that a fresh finding of a protection was required, relying on *St. Pierre and Meloche et al. v. R.C. C.A.S. for Essex County* (1977), 27 R.F.L. 266 (Ont. Div. Ct.). Finally the court discounted the importance of an existing interim custody order as between the parents, the result of

divorce proceedings, where a Crown wardship order was made under the *Child Welfare Act.*

M.M. v. B.M. et al (1982), 37 O.R. (2d) 120 (Co. Ct.).
This is an appeal from a Provincial Court decision which terminated a Crown wardship order and effected a return of the child to the parents under Society supervision.

On appeal the Provincial Court decision was reversed. Webb Co. Ct. J. found that the trial judge misdirected himself as to the appropriate test. The test is whether the applicant had demonstrated that a change in status would be in the best interests of the child.

M.M. v. B.M. et al. (1982), 37 O.R. (2d) 716n (C.A.).
On appeal by the parents from the decision above, the appeal was dismissed. The Court of Appeal held that the County Court judge is uniquely empowered under the *Child Welfare Act* s. 43 to hear evidence relating to matters which both precede or were subsequent to the decision under appeal.

The Court of Appeal should exercise great caution before interfering with any finding of fact made by the County Court judge.

M.M. v. B.M. and C.A.S. Metro. Toronto (1982), 30 R.F.L. (2d) 111 (Ont. S.C.).
After the appeal above was disposed of the parents applied to review the wardship. It was held that the initial proceeding was not determined until the appeal was disposed of. Accordingly the parents may apply for review after 6 months have passed from the date of the appeal decision.

Re G. et al. (1978), 30 R.F.L. 224 (N.B. S.C.).
Where two days intervene between the expiry of one wardship order and the renewing of that order so as to effect an extension, such interruption shall cause the court to lose jurisdiction to extend. This court made this determination subject to the statutory condition that the temporary wardship aggregate could be no greater than 24 months.

Re S. et al. and C.C.A.S. of Metro. Toronto (1983), 42 O.R. (2d) 602 (Prov. Ct.).
Where an appeal of a wardship order is pending, an application for status review is to be stayed until the appeal is dealt with by determination or abandonment.

Re G.M. and R.M. (1978), 20 O.R. (2d) 378 (Div. Ct.).
In considering whether to continue or to terminate a supervision order, the court is not to consider whether the original order ought to have been made. The court is to consider what is in the child's best interests.

Re K. and C.A.S. Kenora (1984), 23 A.C.W.S. (2d) 556 (Ont. Prov. Ct.). On review of a supervision order the court is permitted to make an interim order for temporary care and custody of the child pending completion of the hearing.

S. 60(3): Child Placed Outside Jurisdiction, Under Supervision

(3)   Where a child is the subject of an order for society supervision under subsection 53(1), clauses (2)(a) and (c) also apply to the society that has jurisdiction in the county or district in which the parent or other person with whom the child is placed resides.

The equivalent provision under the *Child Welfare Act* was at s. 32(3).

COMMENTARY:

Under the new legislation, where a child has been placed, under a supervision order, with a person outside of the jurisdiction of the society in whose favour the order was made, then that outside society has a duty under s. 60(2)(a) and (c) to bring a review application before the expiry of the supervision order and may do so at any time.

This new legislation is silent as to whether the original society may still be able to apply for review and if so, in what jurisdiction the review is to be launched. Presumably, consideration as to the "preponderance of convenience" referred to in s. 44(3) would apply.

The *Child Welfare Act* s. 32(3) was permissive in that it gave jurisdiction to the court where the child had been placed. It also remained silent on whether the court hearing the original protection application continued to possess jurisdiction.

S. 60(4): Others Applying to Review Child's Status

(4)   An application for review of a child's status may be made on notice to the society by,
   (a)   the child, where the child is at least twelve years of age;
   (b)   any parent of the child, subject to subsection (5);
   (c)   the person with whom the child was placed under an order for society supervision; or
   (d)   where the child is an Indian or a native person, a representative chosen by the child's band or native community.

The equivalent provisions in the *Child Welfare Act* were at ss. 32(4), 37(2) and 38(1).

COMMENTARY:

While s. 60(4) places no restriction on *when* a status review application can be commenced, it must be read in conjunction with s. 60(7) which, basically, requires the elapse of six months from:

(a)   the making of the original order; or
(b)   the most recent status review disposition; or
(c)   the disposition or abandonment of any appeal from (a) or (b),

before an application for a status review can be made. Here, the individual paragraphs of s. 60(4) are examined in turn. All, of course, are subject to the time-restriction of subsection (7).

S. 60(4)(a)

Under s. 60(4) an application can be made for a status review by:

(a)   the child, where he or she is more than 12 years old. However, if the child is a Crown ward and has been placed for the purpose of adoption, and continues to reside at that placement, the question arises as to whether the child can apply for a review of the Crown wardship given the wording of s. 60(9), which states:

   No *person* or society shall make application under this section where the child,
   (a)   is a Crown ward;
   (b)   has been placed in a person's home by the society or by a Director for the purpose of adoption under Part VII; and
   (c)   still resides in that person's home.

S. 60(4)(b)

Under this clause, any parent of the child may bring a status review application. If the child is a Crown ward and has lived with the same foster parents continuously for two years preceding the application, then the parent must receive the leave of the court to bring the application. (see s. 60(5), *infra*). There are no guidelines for the court in deciding under what circumstances such leave ought to be granted.

In order to determine whether the applicant qualifies as a "parent", reference should be made to the definition at s. 37(d), discussed earlier.

S. 60(4)(c)

This provides that, where a child is the subject of a supervision order, the person with whom the child is placed may apply for review. This is the equivalent of s. 32(4) of the *Child Welfare Act.*

S. 60(4)(d)

Where the child is an Indian or a native person, then a representative of the child's band or native community may apply for status review.
    This clause is without a *Child Welfare Act* equivalent.

S. 60(5): Leave to Apply Where Crown Ward Resided with Same Foster Parent for Two Years

> (5)   Where the child is a Crown ward and has lived with the same foster parent continuously during the two years immediately before the application, an application under subsection (4) shall not be made by any parent of the child without the court's leave.

There was no equivalent subsection in the *Child Welfare Act.*

COMMENTARY:

Where a child is a Crown ward and has resided with the same foster parents continuously for two years preceding the application, then the parent must obtain leave of the court before bringing an application for review.
    There are no statutory guidelines indicating when leave ought to be granted or refused.

CASE LAW: S. 60(5):

Cox v. C.A.S. Metro. Toronto (1979), 23 O.R. (2d) 351, 8 R.F.L. (2d) 391 (Ont. Prov. Ct.).
Once a Crown ward has been placed for adoption there is no jurisdiction to order access.

Re Lyttle, [1971] 3 O.R. 129, 21 D.L.R. (3d) 639n (C.A.), varied (1973), S.C.R. 568, 34 D.L.R. (3d) 127.
Where a child born out of wedlock was made a Crown ward without notice to the putative father, the court ordered that the father be given notice of any application to adopt.

S. 60(6): Society to Give Notice of Status Review

> (6)   A society making an application under subsection (2) or receiving notice of an application under subsection (4) shall give notice of the application to,
>   (a)   the child, subject to subsections 39(4) and (5) (notice to child);
>   (b)   the child's parent, unless the child is a Crown ward and is sixteen years of age or older;

(c)   the person with whom the child was placed under an order for society supervision;
(d)   a foster parent who has cared for the child continuously during the six months immediately before the application;
(e)   where the child is an Indian or a native person, a representative chosen by the child's band or native community; and
(f)   a Director, if the child is a Crown ward.

The comparable provisions in the *Child Welfare Act* were at ss. 32, 37 and 38.

COMMENTARY:

There are only relatively minor substantive changes in the notice requirements between the old and the new Acts.

S. 60(7), (8): No Status Review Within Six Months of Prior Determination; and an Exception

(7)   No application shall be made under subsection (4) within six months of,
(a)   the making of the original order under subsection 53(1);
(b)   the disposition of a previous application by any person under subsection (4); or
(c)   the final disposition or abandonment of an appeal from an order referred to in clause (a) or (b),
whichever is the latest.
(8)   Subsection (7) does not apply where,
(a)   the child is a society ward or the subject of an order for society supervision, or the child is a Crown ward and an order for access has been made under subsection 55(2); and
(b)   the court is satisfied that a major element of the plan for the child's care that the court applied in its decision is not being carried out.

The equivalent provisions of the *Child Welfare Act* were at ss. 32(4), 37(2), 38(1), 38(2).

COMMENTARY:

The new provisions stipulate that a review of a supervision order, society wardship order, or Crown wardship order may not be commenced until six months from:

(a)   the making of the original order;

(b)   a previous status review determination; or

(c)   the determination of any appeal whichever is the latest.

Where a child is a Crown ward and resides in a person's home for the purpose of adoption, no status review is permitted under s. 60(9).

The above referred-to time limits do not apply if both of the two conditions of s. 60(8) apply:

(a) (1) the child is a society ward; or

　　(2) the child is the subject of supervision; or

　　(3) the child is a Crown ward to whom access has been ordered, and

(b)   a major element of the plan for the child's care, and applied by the court in its decision, is not being fulfilled.

It remains to be seen what constitutes a "major element" of the "plan for the child's care that the court applied in its decision", and to what extent the court must be "satisfied" that such "element" is not being carried out before the court will allow a status review in less than the six-month period.

The old legislation provided for review of a supervision or society wardship order after the expiry of six months from the making of the order or the disposition of any previous review, whichever was later. In the case of Crown wards, under the old Act, a parent or the child could apply for status review after the expiry of six months from the making of the order of the last review under s. 38(1). The society could apply at any time to review a Crown wardship order under s. 38(2).

S. 60(9): No Review Where Child Placed for Adoption

(9)   **No person or society shall make an application under this section where the child,**

(a)   **is a Crown ward;**

(b)   **has been placed in a person's home by the society or by a Director for the purpose of adoption under Part VII; and**

(c)   **still resides in that person's home.**

There was no equivalent provision under the *Child Welfare Act.*

COMMENTARY:

This new section, simply stated, stipulates that a review of a Crown wardship order may not be made where the Crown ward has been placed for adoption in a person's home and the ward continues to reside in that person's home at the time of the contemplated review application. A partial exception to this restriction could result from a review by a Director set out in s. 62. (See also ss. 138 and 139).

The general thrust is similar to the former legislation, where a Crown wardship order could not be reviewed under a status review application "where the child has been placed for the purpose of adoption in the home of a person who has been approved by a society or by a Director as a suitable person to adopt the child, and while the child is residing in that person's home". (*Child Welfare Act*, s. 38(7)).

The objective of these provisions remains the same: the protection and insulation of the adoptive family, such that emotional and psychological bonds may form without possible threat from the biological parents, or from other persons from the child's past, attempting to disrupt the newly-constituted family unit. This is consistent with s. 154 of the Act.

S. 60(10): Interim Care and Custody upon Status Review

(10) **Where an application is made under this section, the child shall remain in the care and custody of the person or society having charge of the child, until the application is disposed of, unless the court is satisfied that the child's best interests require a change in the child's care and custody.**

The equivalent provision in the *Child Welfare Act* was at ss. 37(6) and 37(9).

COMMENTARY:

Under the new Act the existing care and custody arrangement is to be maintained throughout the period required for status review of a supervision order, or a society or Crown wardship order. There was no equivalent provision in the old legislation with respect to supervision orders.

This *status quo* requirement holds "unless the court is satisfied that the child's best interests require a change in the child's care and custody." The test under the *Child Welfare Act* was similar insofar as it required the *status quo* "unless cause is shown why a change in the arrangements for the care and custody of the child should be made."

While the wording has changed, the onus, in practice, will remain the same. There will remain a heavy onus on the party seeking to alter the care arrangements during the period of time in which the status review is being conducted.

The new legislation offers additional guidance insofar as the court is to consider the child's best interests, which will require the court to consider the factors enumerated at s. 37(3).

S. 61(1) and (2): Court's Powers to Vary

(1) Where an application for review of a child's status is made under section 60, the court may, in the child's best interests,
  (a) vary or terminate the original order made under subsection 53(1), including a term or condition or a provision for access that is part of the order;
  (b) order that the original order terminate on a specified future date; or
  (c) make a further order or orders under section 53.

(2) Where a child has been made a Crown ward under paragraph 3 of subsection 53(1), the court shall not make an order for society wardship under subsection (1).

The equivalent provisions of the *Child Welfare Act* were at ss. 32(1), 37(1) and 38(2).

COMMENTARY:

The powers provided to a court upon status review are now broader than those delineated under the *Child Welfare Act's* equivalent ss. 32(1), 37(1) and 38(2).

Contrary to the provisions of the old Act, the new s. 61(1)(b) expressly states that the court, upon review, can specify a future date upon which the original order will terminate. Presumably this would be some date sooner than the original order would otherwise expire.

The *Child Welfare Act* s. 37(1) specified that the court could not make a further society wardship order that resulted in the child being in the continuous care of the society in excess of 24 months. This same provision is set out at s. 66(1) of the new Act.

The legislation remains the same in the respect that Crown wards cannot be made society wards upon review.

The court retains the authority to vary any term or condition of a supervision order, society wardship order or Crown wardship order, including granting or terminating the right to access.

CASE LAW: S. 61(1) and (2):

C.A.S. Hamilton – Wentworth and C.F. (1980), 14 R.F.L. (2d) 167, 27 O.R. (2d) 168 (Ont. Unified Fam. Ct.).
On an application to dismiss an application to terminate an order of Crown wardship on the grounds that the application to terminate was premature (having been brought outside of the six month period since the order was made but within six months on the last appeal taken) the application was dismissed and the application to terminate was not premature. The six-month period during which no applica-

tion to vary is to be considered by a court runs from the date the order is first made as opposed to the date of the last appeal disposition.

Bailey and C.A.S. for the Dist. of Parry Sound (1979), 22 O.R. (2d) 95 (H.C.J.).
Where a Children's Aid Society had launched an appeal from a District Court order which varied a Crown wardship order to a ten-month society wardship order, the society had taken no steps prior to the appeal. On application by return of a writ of *habeas corpus Ad Subjiciendum* the court ruled that the appeal by the society did not stay the District Court order which had by the time of hearing before the court expired without either party applying for a further judicial determination. The court considered that to hold otherwise "would make a terminal date in any custody order totally meaningless; particularly if there was no dispute". Hence, the society wardship order having expired the child was directed to be returned to the parent.

C.C.A.S. v. J. (1981), 24 R.F.L. (2d) 195 (Ont. Unified Fam. Ct.)
In a status review of a society wardship order in which the order sought is one of Crown wardship, the determination to be made is what is in the best interests of the child.

S. 61(3): Criteria for Status Review Variation

(3) Before making an order under subsection (1), the court shall consider,
   (a) whether the grounds on which the original order was made still exist;
   (b) whether the plan for the child's care that the court applied in its decision is being carried out;
   (c) what services have been provided or offered under this Act to the person who had charge of the child immediately before the intervention under this Part;
   (d) whether the person is satisfied with those services;
   (e) whether the society is satisfied that the person has co-operated with the society and with any person or agency providing services;
   (f) whether the person or the child requires further services;
   (g) whether, where immediate termination of an order has been applied for but is not appropriate, a future date for termination of the order can be estimated; and
   (h) what is the least restrictive alternative that is in the child's best interests.

The comparable provision in the *Child Welfare Act* was at ss. 32(1), 35(1), 37(1).

COMMENTARY:
Under the former legislation the test was whether it was in the best interests of the child to continue, vary or terminate an existing order. This test has been replaced by a consideration of the factors listed above.

In summary, the court when reviewing a previous order, considers whether the condition which gave rise to the original order continues to exist, and evaluates the effectiveness of the plan proposed at the time the original order was made.

There continues to be an emphasis on the least restrictive alternative that is in the child's best interests. This will entail a reconsideration of the parameters set out in s. 53(3), (4) (and s. 53(5) if the child is an Indian or native person).

A review of the considerations set out in s. 53(3) establishes a continuing obligation on the service provider to ensure that the plan on which the original order was based is being carried out, and to be in a position to explain any delay in, or alteration to, the plan.

SECTION 62. DIRECTOR'S ANNUAL REVIEW OF CROWN WARDS

This section provides for a review, at least annually, of the status of every child who is a Crown ward.

S. 62

(1)   A Director or a person authorized by a Director shall, at least once during each calendar year, review the status of every child,
    (a)   who is a Crown ward;
    (b)   who was a Crown ward throughout the immediately preceding twenty-four months; and
    (c)   whose status has not been reviewed under this section or under section 61 during that time.

(2)   After a review under subsection (1), the Director may direct the society to make an application for review of the child's status under subsection 60(2) or give any other direction that, in the Director's opinion, is in the child's best interests.

The equivalent provision in the *Child Welfare Act* was at s. 39.

COMMENTARY:

The Director or his or her designate has an obligation to review, at least once per year, the status of every child who had been a Crown ward in the preceding 24 month period.

Where the results of such review require, the Director may:

(a) direct the society in whose care the Crown ward is to apply for a review of the child's status under s. 60(2);

(b) give any other direction consistent with the child's best interests.

The review provided for in s. 62 is not a status review in the sense that a review under ss. 60 and 61 is. No criteria are set down for a review under s. 62; no substantive change to the earlier order is provided for; in fact the most a Director can do toward effecting a status change, is to direct the society to apply for a review. In comparison with its *Child Welfare Act* counterpart at s. 39, this new section widens the Director's scope of authority by inserting the words, "... or give any other directions ...". This is authority which the Director may exercise concomitantly with s. 73 so as to bear on placement. This should not be taken to mean a change in status.

SECTION 63. INVESTIGATION BY A JUDGE

This section makes a wide-ranging provision for a public inquiry into any matter concerning a child in a society's care, or the administration of Part III.

S. 63

(1) The Minister may appoint a judge of the Supreme Court, District Court, Unified Family Court, Provincial Court (Family Division), Provincial Court (Criminal Division), Provincial Offences Court or Provincial Court (Civil Division) to investigate a matter relating to,
(a) a child in a society's care; or
(b) the proper administration of this Part,
and the judge shall conduct the investigation and make written report to the Minister.

(2) For the purposes of an investigation under subsection (1), the judge has the powers of a commission under Part II of the *Public Inquiries Act,* and that Part applies to the investigation as if it were an inquiry under that Act.

The equivalent provision in the *Child Welfare Act* was at s. 3(1)(2).

COMMENTARY:

With only minor modification to bring the old provision in line with new statutory provisions at s. 63(2) and to establish (at s. 63(1)) a wider array of judicial officers who might undertake the intended inquiry, the content remains the same as before.

SECTION 64. SOCIETY REVIEW PROCEDURE

This section requires every society to have a written procedure for internal review of a complaint by any person.

S. 64

    (1)   **A society shall establish a written review procedure, which shall be approved by a Director, for hearing and dealing with complaints by any person regarding services sought or received from the society, and shall make the review procedure available to any person on request.**

    (2)   **A review procedure established under subsection (1), shall include an opportunity for the person making the complaint to be heard by the society's board of directors.**

    (3)   **A person who makes a complaint and is not satisfied with the response of the society's board of directors may have the matter reviewed by a Director.**

There was no equivalent provision in the *Child Welfare Act.*

COMMENTARY:

This section should be read concomitantly with s. 105 of the Act. Section 64 provides that each children's aid society must establish a review procedure, to be approved by a Director. The procedure is to deal with the complaints of any person about society services. These points are significant:

(1)   the procedure must be in writing;

(2)   it shall cover complaints about society services sought or received;

(3)   it must be available to any person.

    The initial review steps will presumably be through society administration, but ultimate access to the society board of directors is provided at s. 64(2). Beyond access to the board, the complaint may still be put to the Director. The powers of the Director are prescribed at s. 17. The ultimate authority of the minister to deal with a society unprepared to do what is necessary to correct a circumstance it is obliged to correct are likewise prescribed at ss. 22 to 24.

SECTION 65. APPEALS

This section provides the ground rules governing appeals against any order made under Part III, except an assessment order.

S. 65

(1) An appeal from a court's order under this Part may be made to the District Court by,
   (a) the child, if the child is entitled to participate in the proceeding under subsection 39(6) (child's participation);
   (b) any parent of the child;
   (c) the person who had charge of the child immediately before intervention under this Part;
   (d) a Director or local director; or
   (e) where the child is an Indian or a native person, a representative chosen by the child's band or native community.

(2) Subsection (1) does not apply to an order for an assessment under section 50.

(3) Where a decision regarding the care and custody of a child is appealed under subsection (1), execution of the decision shall be stayed for the ten days immediately following service of the notice of appeal on the court that made the decision, and where the child is in the society's custody at the time the decision is made, the child shall remain in the care and custody of the society until,
   (a) the ten day period of the stay has expired; or
   (b) an order is made under subsection (4).
   whichever is earlier.

(4) The District Court may, in the child's best interests, make a temporary order for the child's care and custody pending final disposition of the appeal, except an order placing the child in a place of secure custody as defined in Part IV (Young Offenders) or a place of secure temporary detention as defined in that Part that has not been designated as a place of safety, and the District Court may, on any party's motion before the final disposition of the appeal, vary or terminate the order or make a further order.

(5) No extension of the time for an appeal shall be granted where the child has been placed for adoption under Part VII (Adoption).

(6) The District Court may receive further evidence relating to events after the appealed decision.

(7) An appeal under this section shall be heard in the county or district in which the order appealed from was made.

(8) Section 41 (hearings private, etc.) applies with necessary modifications to an appeal under this section.

The equivalent provision in the *Child Welfare Act* was at s. 43.

COMMENTARY:

In the commentary below, the provisions of the new Act and the principal changes that have been made, are examined under the headings: (i) who may appeal, (ii) restrictions, (iii) the place of appeal, and (iv) the procedures of appeal.

(i) *Who may appeal:*   The persons specified at s. 65(1)(a) through (e) may initiate an appeal. This differs from the provisions of the *Child Welfare Act* in only two respects. The new Act extends the child's right to appeal to give such rights to any child who is entitled to participate in the proceeding (see s. 65(1)(a) and s. 39(6)). This would normally refer to a child 12 or more, in whose case the court is satisfied that no emotional harm would ensue from the hearing; it would appear also to apply to a child who "has legal representation in a proceeding" (s. 39(6)). The counsel may, in such case, have the task of determining the appeal's merit without the benefit of express instructions from the client.

Secondly, the new Act, at s. 65(1)(e), adds to the list to provide for the child who is an Indian or a native person. In such case, "a representative chosen by the child's band or native community" may initiate an appeal. This is consistent, given the party status accorded to such a representative at s. 39(1)(4).

Since this section covers appeals against "any order made under Part III", it should be noticed that the definition of "an order" in the new Act (s. 3(1)(21)) includes "a refusal to make an order." Section 43(1) of the *Child Welfare Act* provided for an appeal against a decision refusing an order. The definition in the new Act makes this specific direction unnecessary, and the right of appeal presumably still applies against such a refusal.

(ii) *Restrictions on appeal:*   No appeal lies from any order for assessment under s. 50. This is a carry-over from s. 43(1) of the *Child Welfare Act.*

Where the appeal is made against an order under s. 53 (supervision, society or Crown wardship or the combined wardship supervision order), or against a temporary placement order under s. 42(2) or s. 47(2), the execution of the order will be stayed for ten days after service of the notice of appeal on "the court that made the decision." (See s. 65(3)). Where the child who is the subject of the order, is in a society's custody, the child shall remain there until:

(a) the ten-day period of the stay has expired; or
(b) a temporary order for care and custody is made by the appeal court,

whichever is the shorter period (see s. 65(3)). This is consistent with the predecessor provision under the *Child Welfare Act* at s. 43(2).

As was the case under s. 43(3) of the old Act, the temporary custody order which the appeal court may consider pending the appeal's disposition at s. 65(4) is subject to specific directions:

(1) the test to be employed by the court is "the child's best interests";
(2) the court may not place a child in certain facilities. Under the new Act, these are:
    (a) a place of secure custody;
    (b) a place of secure temporary detention that has not been designated as a place of safety;

such temporary placement order may be varied or terminated or a new order made, prior to the disposition of the appeal.

A society involved in an appeal, (unless, to its satisfaction, a child is at home), will normally bring an application to secure an order under s. 65(6). Once beyond the ten-day period provided for at s. 65(3), however, if the society has failed to secure a temporary order sanctioning its continued custodial care, the child must be returned to the person entitled. The onus will remain upon the applicant (in most cases the society) seeking the temporary order for custody.

Where a child has been placed for adoption, the court may not extend the time for appeal. The appeal periods are prescribed in the Rules of Civil Procedure. Thus, where a Crown wardship order is made at trial, an appellant (most likely a parent) is obliged to move quickly within the prescribed appeal periods. Once outside an appeal period, a society has a legal obligation to "make all reasonable efforts to secure the adoption" of any Crown ward. (See s. 134(1)). A similar provision was found at s. 68 of the *Child Welfare Act.*

(iii) *The place of the appeal:* An appeal is to the District Court and shall be disposed of in the county or district of the place where the order was made. (See s. 65(1) and s. 65(7)). This is akin to the old law provisions (see s. 43(1)).

(iv) *Procedures:* All the provisions of s. 41 relative to the privacy of hearings, apply by virtue of s. 65(8). This is new.

The appeal court under both old (s. 43(8)) and new law (s. 65(6)) has the discretion to permit the introduction of new evidence. While not as specific as s. 43(8) (that such evidence "may be received by affidavit, oral examination or as may be directed . . .") the court has authority within its discretion, to admit new evidence and to direct the manner in which such evidence shall be presented. This is in contrast to the *Child Welfare Act* at s. 43(8), which spelled out the scope of the type of evidence (". . . evidence relating to matters both preceding and subsequent to the making of the decision . . ."). The absence is not fatal. The appeal court, given the broad latitude at s. 65(6), may admit what, in its discretion, is appropriate.

CASE LAW: S. 65(4)

C.C.A.S. v. O. et al. (1983), 26 A.C.W.S. (2d) 138 (Ont. Co. Ct.).
Where an order is under appeal, the appeal court has the jurisdiction to make a temporary order pending disposition of the appeal based on what is in the best interests of the child.

Re Genereux and C.C.A.S. of Metro. Toronto (1985), 53 O.R. (2d) 163 (C.A.).
Appeal from District Court which refused to hear further evidence on the appeal from Family Court. The District Court, under Child Welfare Act s. 43(8) refused to allow further evidence on the basis that it could not find an error in law allowing him to hear further evidence. The Court of Appeal held that s. 43(8) is not to be so narrowly interpreted; the Appeal Court is given a broad discretion. The judge on appeal, bearing in mind that he is dealing with the welfare of children, may determine that he will exercise his discretion and will hear further evidence so long as it is relevant to a consideration of the best interests of the child.

SECTION 66. EXPIRY OF ORDERS

The section sets a maximum limit on the time a child can be kept as a society ward. The limit is 24 months.

S. 66

(1) Subject to subsection (3), the court shall not make an order under this Part that results in a child being a society ward for a continuous period exceeding twenty-four months.

(2) In the calculation of the 24-month period referred to in subsection (1), time during which a child is in a society's care,

    (a) under an agreement made under subsection 29(1), or 30(1) (temporary care or special needs agreement) of Part II (Voluntary Access to Services); or

    (b) under a temporary order made under clause 47(2)(d), shall be counted.

(3) Where the twenty-four month period referred to in subsection (1) expires, and,

    (a) an appeal of an order made under subsection 53(1) has

been commenced and is not yet finally disposed of; or

(b) the court has adjourned a hearing under section 61 (status review), the period shall be deemed to be extended until the appeal has been finally disposed of and any new hearing ordered on appeal has been completed or an order has been made under section 61, as the case may be.

The equivalent provisions in the *Child Welfare Act* were at ss. 30(2), 37(1), 43(5) and 37(3).

COMMENTARY:

A child may not, subject to two specified exceptions, remain in continuous care of a society for a period in excess of 24 months. This limit must be taken into account when any order is made placing the child in a society's custody. Under subsection (2) such order is limited to 24 months, *including* time the child may have spent under:

(1) any agreements made under s. 29 or s. 30;
(2) any temporary orders for care made under s. 47(2)(d) (Adjournment).

The time under s. 66(2)(a) stems from the start of any agreement. The agreement may have resulted from the parties making that arrangement under circumstances set out at s. 42(1)(c). The clock starts from the date of the agreement and does *not* include the five days immediately prior to the initial court date.

Likewise where the period involves s. 66(2)(b), the clock ticks from the date of the first temporary placement under s. 47(2)(d) and excludes the period of up to five days from apprehension, until the child was delivered to the court.

The two exceptions relate to:

(1) the time from commencement to disposition of an appeal under s. 65 to a s. 53 order; or
(2) the time from commencement to disposition of a status review under s. 61.

Under either circumstance, where the society wardship would otherwise end by virtue of the 24 month limitation, it is "deemed" extended under s. 66(3) until:

(1) the appeal is disposed of, or any new hearing directed by the appeal has been completed;
(2) the completion of any status review under s. 61.

CASE LAW S. 66(1)

Re McDonald (1983), 23 A.C.W.S. (2d) 418 (Ont. Prov. Ct.).
A child may not remain in care for a period in excess of 24 months, whether by combination of agreements or extensions of orders or adjournments.

SECTION 67. EXPIRY OF ORDERS

All orders under Part III expire upon the child's marriage or 18th birthday. For a Crown ward, a society *may* continue care and maintenance beyond that point.

S. 67

(1)   An order under this Part expires when the child who is the subject of the order,
(a)   attains the age of eighteen years; or
(b)   marries,
whichever comes first.
(2)   Where an order for Crown wardship expires under subsection (1), the society may, with a Director's approval, continue to provide care and maintenance for the former Crown ward in accordance with the regulations.

The equivalent provision in the *Child Welfare Act* was s. 42.

COMMENTARY:

The old and new legislation are very similar in this respect. Any order under Part III expires upon the marriage or the 18th birthday of the child, whichever comes first.

Under s. 67(2) a society is permitted to continue service to a Crown ward after either condition in s. 67(1). In the past, such continuation of services has included:

(1)   foster care;
(2)   allowance for independent room and board;
(3)   cost of tuition for post-secondary education; and
(4)   payment of ancillary living or education expenses,

to a maximum age of 21 years. Such a decision by a society continues to require the approval of the Director.

While s. 42 of the *Child Welfare Act* specified within the statute at (a) and (b) the conditions for extension of service, the new Act omits this but refers to regulations. Further, the new Act explicitly allows such extension of service following either the marriage or the 18th birthday of the Crown ward. The *Child Welfare Act* provided only for the case where "a wardship expires as a result of a Crown ward attaining the age of eighteen years." In addition two conditions for such extension of service which existed under the old Act at s. 42, namely:

(a)   that the child be enrolled as a full-time student;
(b)   that the child be mentally or physically incapacitated,

are absent in the new Act.

SECTION 68. DUTY TO REPORT ABUSE

Every person is obliged to report to a society, cases where it is believed that a child is in need of protection. The professional is obliged to report to a society suspected abuse. The important definition of "abuse" in terms of the need for protection, is introduced in this section.

S. 68

(1)   In this section and in sections 69, 70 and 71, "to suffer abuse", when used in reference to a child, means to be in need of protection within the meaning of clause 37(2)(a), (c), (e), (f) or (h).

(2)   A person who believes on reasonable grounds that a child is or may be in need of protection shall forthwith report the belief and the information upon which it is based to a society.

(3)   Despite the provisions of any other Act, a person referred to in subsection (4) who, in the course of his or her professional or official duties, has reasonable grounds to suspect that a child is or may be suffering or may have suffered abuse shall forthwith report the suspicion and the information on which it is based to a society.

(4)   Subsection (3) applies to every person who performs professional or official duties with respect to a child, including,

   (a)   a health care professional, including a physician, nurse, dentist, pharmacist and psychologist;
   (b)   a teacher, school principal, social worker, family counsellor, priest, rabbi, clergyman, operator or employee of a day nursery and youth and recreation worker;
   (c)   a peace officer and a coroner;
   (d)   a solicitor; and
   (e)   a service provider and an employee of a service provider.

(5)   In clause (4) (b), "youth and recreation worker" does not include a volunteer.

(6)   A society that obtains information that a child in its care and custody is or may be suffering or may have suffered abuse shall forthwith report the information to a Director.

(7)   This section applies although the information reported may be confidential or privileged, and no action for making the report shall be instituted against a person who acts in accordance with subsection (2) or (3) unless the person acts maliciously or without reasonable grounds for the belief or suspicion, as the case may be.

(8)   Nothing in this section abrogates any privilege that may exist between a solicitor and his or her client.

The equivalent provisions of the *Child Welfare Act* were at s. 49.

COMMENTARY:

The Concept of Abuse:

(i)   *The Old Act:*

Under the *Child Welfare Act*, "abuse" of a child was defined at s. 47(1)(a) through (c), as a condition of physical harm, malnutrition or mental ill-health, or sexual molestation. Abuse was not specifically defined in terms of the need for "protection" either in these paragraphs or at s. 19(1)(b) of the old Act.

Sections 47 and 48 of the *Child Welfare Act* describe other situations relating to a child which, in addition to abuse as defined at s. 47(1), would result in a hearing "as though the child had been brought before the court as a child apparently in need of protection." (See s. 47(3) and s. 48(2)). The references in those two sections were to:

(1)   abandonment or desertion of a child (see s. 47(2)), but see also s. 19(1)(b)(ii); and

(2)   leaving a child without reasonable provision for the child's supervision, care or safety (see s. 48(1)) for which an age presumption applied at s. 48(3).

(ii)   *The New Act:*

The new Act defines "abuse" in such way as to equate the meaning of "to suffer abuse" and "to be in need of protection" under specific paragraphs in s. 37. In particular, at s. 68(1), abuse is defined to mean any of the conditions of protection which are defined at:

(1) s. 37(2)(a) – physical harm;

(2) s. 37(2)(c) – sexual molestation or exploitation;
(3) s. 37(2)(e) – need for medical treatment where parent will not
          provide;
(4) s. 37(2)(f) – emotional harm; and
(5) s. 37(2)(h) – need for treatment for mental, emotional or de-
          velopmental condition.

Thus, five different protection situations are summed up in the phrase "to suffer abuse", which becomes the basis on which the Act sets up the obligation to report, as imposed upon professionals.

Each of the clauses referred to in s. 37(2), when defining the need for "protection", includes as an ingredient, the words ". . . the person having charge of the child . . ." which heightens the aspect of control expected by the caretaker on the "abuse" definition. The absence in s. 68(2) of words which were found in s. 49(2) of the *Child Welfare Act* as an ingredient, *i.e.* "by a person who has or has had charge of the child" in reference to the above, really is, as a result, insignificant.

(iii) Reporting Obligations:

Section 68(2) requires persons who "believe" that a child is in need of protection as defined in the wider sense in the Act, to report it forwith to a children's aid society. The former Act, at s. 49(1), likewise required persons having information of protection, or of abuse to a child, to report it. This is the general reporting obligation imposed on everyone, including professionals.

Perhaps to underscore the serious implications of such reporting, the provisions of s. 68(2) point the obligation to where there is a belief "on reasonable grounds." This language is lacking in the old Act at s. 49(1), though it does appear in that Act when applied to the person who might have such information arising "in the course of the person's professional or official duties." This suggests a narrowing of the general reporting obligation because the standard against which that obligation is measured, is raised.

Both Acts place emphasis upon the obligation of the "professional" person to report "abuse", as defined in the respective Acts. Where professionals are concerned, the words "believes on reasonable grounds" (which had been applied to "persons" in subsection (2)) become "has reasonable grounds to suspect", in subsection (3). Similarly, "belief" changes to "suspicion", though the possible significance of the use of different terminology is not clear.

What distinguishes s. 68 is the inclusion of a specific list of persons who are in the category of "professional" or "official" and upon whom falls the duty to report their "suspicion and the information on which it is based." These persons are listed at s. 68(4)(a) through (e), though the list is not presented as being exhaustive.

Two qualifications pertain to professionals. The "youth and recreation worker" in s. 68(4)(b) does not include a volunteer. (see s. 68(5)). However, while that might remove such a person from the obligation to report a "suspicion", it does not exclude that person from the general reporting obligation that would apply to every person to report "belief and information" on reasonable grounds of abuse, as imposed by s. 68(1).

The second qualification relates to the solicitor whose client may disclose information that would be the subject of the solicitor-client privilege. The privilege is not disturbed. (see s. 68(8)).

As a result of these obligations imposed on professionals, parties to various proceedings involving the interests of children, should appreciate that what they might believe to be a privileged disclosure may result in a report to a society. For example in an assessment under s. 30 of the *Children's Law Reform Act* S.O. 1982, c. 20, a psychologist, having interviewed both parents, may, as a result of information received, suspect abuse and be obliged to report it.

Any person reporting such abuse to a society has immunity, provided such reporting was not done "maliciously" or "without reasonable grounds for the belief or suspicion." (see s. 68(7) carried over from s. 49(3) of the *Child Welfare Act*).

There is no express instruction as to how the reporting obligation is discharged. Contacting a children's aid society is probably sufficient. No written report is required.

A children's aid society has a reporting obligation imposed upon it by virtue of s. 68(6). Where information as to abuse comes to its attention, it is obliged to report it to a Director. It would appear that this was inserted to cover circumstances where a child "may be suffering or may have suffered abuse" and this comes to the society's attention through investigations on its own (as opposed to persons reporting it under s. 68(2)). An obligation to report to a Director is triggered.

Perhaps, in addition, the obligation to report directly to a Director, child abuse found by a society on its own was meant to cover occasions outside the limit of s. 71(3), where a society *receives* a child abuse report and must forward it to a Director. In either event, where a society, of its own investigation determines abuse, its reporting obligation is clear.

CASE LAW

S. 68(3) *R. v. Cook* (1983), 46 R.F.L. (2d) 174, 10 O.A.C. 101, revg 37 R.F.L. (2d) 93 (Prov. Ct.).

Section 49(2) which imposes a reporting duty on professionals who suspect abuse sets an objective test of reasonableness in the suspicion of abuse.

Also, it is not sufficient to support the charge that the material constituted reasonable grounds to suspect that child abuse had taken place at some time in the past. It is necessary to show that the child *is* suffering from abuse.

R. v. Stachula (1984), 40 R.F.L. (2d) 184 (Ont. Prov. Ct.)
Considers *R. v. Cook.*

S. 68(8) *Re Cameron* (1977), 27 R.F.L. 205 (B.C. Prov. Ct.).
Where a solicitor was subpoenaed to give evidence of a communication with a child, the solicitor claimed solicitor-client privilege despite express statutory provision that the obligation to give evidence overrode any privilege. The court conducted an extensive review of the law and concluded that the legislation did not expressly abrogate or override the privilege attaching to the solicitor-client privilege and that therefore, it continued to prohibit the solicitor from the giving of evidence of that communication.

SECTION 69. REVIEW TEAMS

This section requires every society to have a "review team." The composition and functions of such teams are set out. They are primarily to review and recommend on cases referred by the society, where a child has suffered abuse.

S. 69

(1) In this section, "review team" means a team established by a society under subsection (2).
(2) Every society shall establish a review team that includes,
    (a) persons who are professionally qualified to perform medical, psychological, developmental, educational or social assessments; and
    (b) at least one legally qualified medical practitioner.
(3) The members of a review team shall choose a chairman from among themselves.
(4) Whenever a society refers the case of a child who may be suffering or may have suffered abuse to its review team, the review team or a panel of at least three of its members, designated by the chairman, shall,
    (a) review the case; and
    (b) recommend to the society how the child may be protected.

(5)   Despite the provisions of any other Act, a person may disclose to a review team or to any of its members information
reasonably required for a review under subsection (4).

(6)   Subsection (5) applies although the information disclosed
may be confidential or privileged and no action for disclosing the information shall be instituted against a person who
acts in accordance with subsection (5), unless the person acts
maliciously or without reasonable grounds.

(7)   Where a society with a review team has information that a
child placed in its care under subsection 47(2) (temporary
care and custody) or subsection 53(1) (order where child in
need of protection) may have suffered abuse, the society
shall not return the child to the care of the person who had
charge of the child at the time of the possible abuse unless,
(a)   the society has,
       (i) referred the case to its review team, and
       (ii) obtained and considered the review team's recom-
       mendations; or
(b)   the court has terminated the order placing the child in
the society's care.

There was no equivalent section in the *Child Welfare Act*.

COMMENTARY:

This section is new. It is designed to provide input from professional
representatives of the community on child abuse cases. The team is
established by each children's aid society. Membership is restricted to
professional persons of the type cited at s. 69(2). However, there is no
express prohibition against membership being drawn from society
employees. This has the potential of being self-defeating if the objective is critical third party advice.

The team's objective is to review and recommend on cases of
abuse referred to it by its children's aid society. Its recommendations
on any case referred to it must set forth means by which "the child
may be protected." (see s. 69(4)).

The statute provides little by way of guidelines as to the actual
operation of the team. The section does provide:

(1)   that there is to be one legally qualified medical practitioner; (s.
69(2)(b));

(2)   that from among its members, it shall select a chairman (*sic*); (s.
69(3));

(3)   that the team may conduct a review by its whole membership or
by a panel of three;

(4)   that persons providing information that would otherwise be
"privileged or confidential" to such a team have protection

against any action for disclosing such information s. 69(6);

(5)   that its recommendations are made to its own society.

The statute gives the team little by way of authority beyond these provisions. This may be a clear indication that it lacks powers to conduct an inquiry, which in any case does not seem to be its mandate. In fact the rationale for the team's existence seems to be to ensure community input, almost as a source of second opinion on the means of protecting a child.

The society to which a team reports has no obligation to accept its recommendations. The obligations of a society seem limited to the direction at s. 69(7):

(a)   to refer certain cases of abuse;

(b)   to obtain and consider the team's recommendations;

and even here it is not a positive obligation but only a precondition to returning the child to his or her former place.

Further, there appears to be no requirement that *all* cases involving abuse or allegations of abuse be referred to the team. Those cases that will be referred are determined by s. 69(7) and will contain these ingredients:

(1)   the child has been placed in the society's care by virtue of a court order under s. 47(2) or s. 53(1); and

(2)   the society has information that the child may have suffered abuse.

Any case with such ingredients where a society wishes to return a child to the person who had charge of the child at the time of the possible abuse, may be referred to the review team. This will not apply in all cases because of s. 69(7)(b). The society is, subject to s. 69(7)(b), prohibited from returning the child to such person until it has satisfied its obligations under s. 69(7)(a) to refer the case to the team and to consider the recommendations of the team.

Termination of an order made under s. 47(2) is most likely to occur at the hearing conducted to determine the application seeking relief at s. 53(1). An order under s. 53(1) is most likely terminated by a review under s. 61. It is noteworthy that a review of both sections discloses no consideration whatsoever of:

(1)   whether any review team reviewed the case; or

(2)   where a team did review the case, what its recommendations were and what action, if any, a society did take, based on such recommendations.

Thus the team's function, while directed to protection of a child who may have suffered abuse, is as a resource to a society and not to a court.

It remains a decision solely within the purview of the society, which cases if any, are referred to the team provided that they encompass the minimum ingredients of s. 69(4).

The team itself has no recourse once its recommendations have been delivered to a society. Whether or not a society does anything beyond considering the recommendations, the team's function is completed. Furthermore, it has no access or recourse to the court process. The only avenue a review team would appear to have, is to report its findings and any dissatisfaction with a society's handling of its report, to the Director.

Section 70. COURT ORDERED ACCESS TO RECORDS

The purpose of this section is to ensure that any record containing information relevant to a child's suffering abuse is made available; and to prevent disclosure of such information which might be harmful to the child or to other persons.

S. 70

(1) In this section, "record" means recorded information, regardless of physical form or characteristics.

(2) A Director or society may make a motion at any time for an order under subsection (3) for the production of a record or part of a record, on notice to the person in possession or control of the record.

(3) Where the court is satisfied that,

   (a) a record contains information that may be relevant to a consideration of whether a child is suffering abuse or is likely to suffer abuse; and

   (b) the person in possession or control of the record has refused to permit the Director or local director to inspect it,

   the court may order that the person produce the record or a specified part of the record for inspection and copying by the Director or local director or a person authorized by one of them or by the court.

(4) In considering whether to make an order under subsection (3), the court may examine the record.

(5) No person who obtains information by means of an order made under subsection (3) shall disclose the information except,

   (a) as specified in the order; and

   (b) in testimony in a proceeding under this Part.

(6) Subject to subsection (7), this section applies despite any

any other Act, but nothing in this section abrogates any privilege that may exist between a solicitor and his or her client.

(7)   Where an application under subsection (2) concerns a record that is a clinical record within the meaning of section 29 of the Mental Health Act, subsection 29 (6) (attending physician's statement, hearing) of that Act applies and the court shall give equal consideration to,

(a)   the matters to be considered under subsection 29 (7) of that Act; and

(b)   the need to protect the child's health and safety.

The equivalent provisions of the *Child Welfare Act* were at s. 50.

COMMENTARY:

The purpose of s. 70, as with its predecessor, is to allow a Director or a society to obtain from any third party, records or information in connection with a child abuse investigation. This remedy is not available to anyone else.

The use of this section is restricted to child abuse cases. The "abuse" definition at s. 68(1) is critical. It is of no use in the course of any "protection" investigation outside the limited content of that definition at s. 37(2)(a), (c), (e), (f) or (h). These cover actual physical harm, actual sexual molestation or exploitation, need for medical treatment, actual emotional harm, or a serious emotional condition respectively. Such third party sources as might not voluntarily provide information by reason of confidentiality or privilege would include, among others:

(1)   a hospital, a mental health or other medical facility;
(2)   a physician;
(3)   a psychologist or other health professional;
(4)   a police or public protection authority.

They would not include the file of a solicitor whose client has provided information or records under the solicitor-client privilege. (s. 70(6)).

The definition of records at s. 70(1) has a broader scope than that meaning ascribed to it at s. 50(1)(a) of the *Child Welfare Act*. It may include:

(1)   writings;
(2)   documents;
(3)   photographs;
(4)   charts;
(5)   sound recording;

(6)   video tape;
(7)   film;
(8)   information recorded or stored by means of any type of device.

This is important. With the wider use by police, and by professionals in the helping services, of the ever advancing technology in communications recording and preservation, including videotaping on abuse cases, access to such records on an investigation is critical. If a third party source refuses to produce relevant records upon request, they must be obtained by application to a court. A motion must demonstrate the existence of certain criteria to a court's satisfaction:

(1)   that the records may be relevant to the matter of abuse;
(2)   that the party in possession has refused a request of the Director or a society to produce for inspection (s. 70(3));

Proof of (1) could be difficult, even though the test is only "may be". The applicant can only speculate on the relevance of its content. The applicant will have to demonstrate the background circumstances of the abuse; suggesting for example, that resort to the third person's services raises a reasonable inference that a need was felt for assistance in dealing with the abuse. The court however, in making its own determination as to relevance, is entitled to view the record. (see s. 70(4)).

Persons obtaining the records by court order from the third party source are subject to the disclosure restrictions imposed at s. 70(5).

The records contemplated by this section escape the confidentiality sanctions as set out at Part VIII, by virtue of s. 163(2)(a) which specifically exempts from its applications an order under s. 70(3).

In considering whether to require disclosure of such records, the court must consider certain tests prescribed at s. 29(6) and (7) of the *Mental Health Act* R.S.O. 1980, c. 262. These tests relate to the likelihood of harm to the treatment or recovery of the patient or of mental or bodily harm that might result to a third person, as a result of disclosure.

The new Act adds a further consideration to be taken into account by the court in the matter of disclosure of psychiatric records relevant to a child abuse case. That is "the need to protect the child's health and safety." (s. 70(7)(b)). The Act directs that in making a determination on the production of such records, the court shall give *equal* consideration to the tests under the *Mental Health Act*, R.S.O. 1980, c. 262 and the test of the child's health and safety. Neither has any greater or less importance than the other. In this, it is notable that the child's "best interests" is not the test, but rather the child's health and safety.

Where the records are clinical records within the meaning of s.

29 of the *Mental Health Act* R.S.O. 1980, c. 262 different rules apply. These are records of a psychiatric facility. They are the subject of very strict conditions as to disclosure, as outlined in s. 29(3), (4) and (5) of the above Act.

CASE LAW: S. 70(7):

Re C.L.M. (1982), 29 R.F.L. (2d) 460 (Ont. Prov. Ct.).
On a Crown wardship application based on the mother's chronic schizophrenic condition the applicant society sought an order to have the mother's psychiatrist who treated her while at a psychiatric facility, give evidence. The court was obliged to consider the implications of s. 29(9)(c) of the *Mental Health Act* R.S.O. 1980, c. 262 and determine, "if it is essential in the interests of justice that the doctor testify". The court found that psychiatric disclosure was "essential" when:

(1) the patient's psychiatric state was the main issue being litigated; and
(2) that issue could not be determined through other evidence. The court directed disclosure.

Re Clarke Institute of Psychiatry and C.C.A.S. Metro. Toronto (1981), 31 O.R. (2d) 486, 119 D.L.R. (3d) 247 (S.C.).
In a protection proceeding, the society subpoenaed clinical records pursuant to the *Mental Health Act*. The physician in charge stated that in his opinion the disclosure of the contents of the records would likely result in harm in the treatment of the patient. The society then brought a s. 50 *Child Welfare Act* motion for an order producing the clinical records. It was held, that in resolving the apparent conflict between the two statutes, where "protection" is the issue, the records may be relevant and the *Mental Health Act* provisions are incorporated by reference into the *Child Welfare Act* and as such it was not necessary to follow the procedure set out in the *Mental Health Act*.

Re C.A.S. of Belleville and M. et al. (1980), 28 O.R. (2d) 795 (Prov. Ct.).
Where a child is placed with a society during a period of adjournment, that society has the power of a "guardian" within the *Education Act* s. 231(11) and as such may consent to the release of school records. Such records are admissible for the purpose of establishing abuse.

SECTIONS 71 and 72. CHILD ABUSE REGISTER

The purpose of these sections is to provide for the setting up of a Child Abuse Register by a Director, and to establish the rules for inclusion or non-inclusion in the register.

S. 71(1): Definitions

(1)   In this section and in section 72,

    (a)   "Director" means the person appointed under subsection (2);

    (b)   "register" means the register maintained under subsection (5);

    (c)   "registered person" means a person identified in the register, but does not include,

        (i) a person who reports to a society under subsection 68(2) or (3) and is not the subject of the report, or

      (ii) the child who is the subject of a report.

The equivalent provision in the *Child Welfare Act* was at s. 52.

COMMENTARY:

There is no meaningful change between this definition section and that of the *Child Welfare Act*. The new legislation stipulates:

(1)   that a child abuse register is to be maintained and also,

(2)   that the child who is the subject of a report does not fall within the definition of a "registered person."

It would appear, from both Acts, that the "registered person" is intended to be the person causing or allowing abuse to occur, though this is not explicitly set down. It does not include the person who has made the report to the society, under s. 68(2) or (3). In fact, the Act is silent on the legislators' intent as to whether "registered person" is meant to include only persons against whom allegations of abuse have been made and have been investigated.

S. 71(2): Director

(2)   The Minister may appoint an employee of the Ministry as Director for the purposes of this section.

There is no equivalent provision under the *Child Welfare Act*.

COMMENTARY:

There would appear to be no change in practice from the old legislation. The new provision simply establishes that there is an identified Director, appointed within the Ministry of Community and Social Services, responsible for the maintenance of an abuse register (s. 71), and for the holding of a hearing concerning the removal of a person's name from the register (s. 72).

S. 71(3): Society to Report Information Concerning Abuse

(3) A society that receives a report under section 68 that a child, including a child in the society's care, is or may be suffering or may have suffered abuse shall forthwith verify the reported information, or ensure that the information is verified by another society, in the manner determined by the Director, and if the information is verified, the society that verified it shall forthwith report it to the Director in the prescribed form.

The equivalent provision in the Child Welfare Act was at s. 52(2).

COMMENTARY:

In determining whether a society is required to verify the information received, reference must be made to s. 68(1), which directs the reader to s. 37(2)(a), (c), (e), (f) or (h), when considering whether the child "is or may be suffering or may have suffered abuse." In short, the clauses refer to physical harm, sexual exploitation, need of medical treatment, emotional harm, or a condition that could seriously impair the child's development.

In contrast with the *Child Welfare Act* s. 49, which limits the society's duty to verify to reported acts of "abandonment, desertion, need of protection, or abuse" (defined in s. 47 as physical harm, malnutrition, mental ill-health or sexual molestation), the new legislation widens the scope of the acts required to be verified by the society.

Further, the society is required to investigate reports received indicating that the child is in one of three possible stages of abuse, that is,

(1) is suffering abuse;
(2) may be suffering abuse; or
(3) may have suffered abuse.

Where a society receives information concerning possible abuse of a child but that child does not fall within the territorial jurisdiction or religious jurisdiction (where there are more than one society), the receiving society is to ensure that the information is verified by the society having jurisdiction.

S. 71(4): Protection from Liability

(4) No action or other proceeding for damages shall be instituted against an officer or employee of a society, acting in good faith, for an act done in the execution or intended execution

of the duty imposed on the society by subsection (3) or for an alleged neglect or default of that duty.

The equivalent provision in the *Child Welfare Act* was at s. 52(2).

COMMENTARY:

The provision is analogous to the second part of s. 52(2) of the *Child Welfare Act*, which protects an employee of a society from civil liability, when acting in the course of employment in investigating a report of abuse.

S. 71(5): Abuse Register

(5)   The Director shall maintain a register in the manner prescribed by the regulations for the purpose of recording information reported to the Director under subsection (3), but the register shall not contain information that has the effect of identifying a person who reports to a society under subsection 68(2) or (3) and is not the subject of the report.

The equivalent section of the *Child Welfare Act* was s. 52(3).

COMMENTARY:

This provision establishes the Child Abuse Register and sets out that the register will be kept in accordance with the regulations passed pursuant to s. 199(d), which empowers the Lieutenant-Governor in Council to prescribe the form in which reports are to be made. It also contains protection against identification of a person who reports abuse to a society and is not the subject of the report.

S. 71(6): Register to Remain Confidential

(6)   Despite the provisions of any other Act, no person shall inspect, remove, alter or permit the inspection, removal or alteration of information maintained in the register, or disclose or permit the disclosure of information that the person obtained from the register, except as this section authorizes.

The equivalent provision in the *Child Welfare Act* was at s. 52(4).

COMMENTARY:

Insofar as s. 71(6) establishes the general confidentiality of the Child Abuse Register, the principle remains the same as in the equivalent s. 52(4) of the *Child Welfare Act*. Differences arise when considering the exceptions listed in subsections (7) through (12).

S. 71(7) to (12): Access to Abuse Register

(7) A person who is,
   (a) a coroner, or a legally qualified medical practitioner or peace officer authorized in writing by a coroner, acting in connection with an investigation or inquest under the *Coroner's Act;* or
   (b) the Official Guardian or the Official Guardian's authorized agent,
   may inspect, remove and disclose information in the register in accordance with his or her authority.

(8) The Minister or the Director may permit,
   (a) a person who is employed by,
    (i) the Ministry,
    (ii) a society, or
    (iii) a recognized child protection agency outside Ontario; or
   (b) a person who is providing or proposes to provide counselling or treatment to a registered person,
   to inspect and remove information in the register and to disclose the information to a person referred to in subsection (7) or to another person referred to in this subsection, subject to such terms and conditions as the Director may impose.

(9) The Minister or the Director may disclose information in the register to a person referred to in subsection (7) or (8).

(10) A person who is engaged in research may, with the Director's written approval, inspect and use the information in the register, but shall not,
   (a) use or communicate the information for any purpose except research, academic pursuits or the compilation of statistical data; or
   (b) communicate any information that may have the effect of identifying a person named in the register.

(11) A child, a registered person or the child's or registered person's solicitor or agent may inspect only the information in the register that refers to the child or registered person.

(12) A legally qualified medical practitioner may, with the Director's written approval, inspect the information in the register that is specified by the Director.

The equivalent subsections in the *Child Welfare Act* were subsections 52 (5), (6), (7), (8), (9).

COMMENTARY:

In summary form the persons allowed access to Abuse Register information are, in the two Acts respectively,

	C.F.S.A.	C.W.A.
1. Coroner	s. 71(7)(a)	s. 52(5)
2. Official Guardian	s. 71(7)(b)	s. 52(5)
3. Ministry, society	s. 71(8)(a)	s. 52(6)1
4. Therapist or registered person	s. 71(8)(b)	s. 52(6)2
5. Researcher	s. 71(10)	s. 52(7)
6. Child, registered person or their agent (see para. below)	s. 71(11)	s. 52(8)
7. A legally qualified medical practitioner	s. 71(12)	s. 52(9)

The only notable change is the addition of the child as a person who may inspect the information referring to the child (s. 71(11)).

S. 71(13): Amendment of Register

> (13) The Director or an employee of the Ministry acting under the Director's authority,
>   (a) shall remove a name from or otherwise amend the register where the regulations require the removal or amendment; and
>   (b) may amend the register to correct an error.

The equivalent provision in the Child Welfare Act was at s. 52(10).

COMMENTARY:

This section authorizes a Director to remove a name, amend or correct a register.

S. 71(14): Child Abuse Register Inadmissible

> (14) The register shall not be admitted into evidence in a proceeding except,
>   (a) to prove compliance or non-compliance with this section;
>   (b) in a hearing or appeal under section 72;
>   (c) in a proceeding under the *Coroner's Act;* or
>   (d) in a proceeding referred to in section 77 (recovery on child's behalf).

The equivalent provision in the *Child Welfare Act* was at s. 52(11).

COMMENTARY:

As between this and the equivalent provision of the old Act, there are no meaningful changes. This provision excludes the admissibility of the Child Abuse Register with the exception of:

(a) proving compliance or non-compliance with s. 71;
(b) a hearing or appeal of the registration of the name;
(c) a coroner's proceeding, or
(d) a proceeding to recover damages on behalf of the abused child.

S. 72(1): Hearing of Validity of Registration

(1) In this section, "hearing" means a hearing held under clause (4)(b).

There is no equivalent provision in the *Child Welfare Act.*

COMMENTARY:

Essentially this provision establishes the process, consequent upon the Director's receiving a request to remove a registered person's name from the register (s. 72(3)). The Director may hold a hearing (s. 72(4)(b)), which will be governed by the *Statutory Powers Procedures Act* R.S.O. 1980, c. 484 (s. 72(6)).

S. 72(2): Notice to Registered Person

(2) Where an entry is made in the register, the Director shall forthwith give written notice to each registered person referred to in the entry indicating that,
   (a) the person is identified in the register;
   (b) the person or the person's solicitor or agent is entitled to inspect the information in the register that refers to or identifies the person; and
   (c) the person is entitled to request that the Director remove the person's name from or otherwise amend the register.

The equivalent provision in the *Child Welfare Act* was at s. 52(12).

COMMENTARY:

The two provisions of the old and new Acts appear to be substantially the same. While s. 52(12) appears to more widely describe those to whom notice is to be given, the new s. 72(2) requires notice to be given to each registered person. It must be inferred that such registered persons will include those suspected or alleged to have inflicted abuse or to be inflicting abuse.

Notice is to be given to each person identified in the register. Such notice is to inform the person that,

(a)   the person is identified in the register;
(b)   the person, or the person's agent, is entitled to inspect the register; and
(c)   the person is entitled to request the name be removed from the register.

S. 72(3): Request to Amend Register

(3)   **A registered person who receives notice under subsection (2) may request that the Director remove the person's name from or otherwise amend the register.**

The equivalent provision in the *Child Welfare Act* was at s. 52(13).

COMMENTARY:

There are no practical distinctions between this provision and its predecessor in the *Child Welfare Act*. Section 72(3) simply establishes the right of the "registered person" to request that the Director remove the person's name from the register.

S. 72(4): Director's Response

(4)   **On receiving a request under subsection (3), the Director may,**
      (a)   **grant the request; or**
      (b)   **hold a hearing, on ten days written notice to the parties, to determine whether to grant or refuse the request.**

The equivalent provision of the *Child Welfare Act* was at s. 52(14).

COMMENTARY:

The former section, s. 52(14) of the *Child Welfare Act* required the Director to hold a hearing "before deciding to refuse the request" to remove the name from the register or otherwise amend it. This very ambiguous direction seems to imply that the Director could grant the request with or *without* the necessity of a hearing, but could only refuse it *with* a hearing. Presumably, after a hearing, the Director could decide to grant the request, although this is not expressly stated. The new provision clarifies this confusion.

S. 72(5): Delegation of Director's Authority

(5)   **The Director may authorize another person to hold a hearing and exercise the Director's powers and duties under subsection (8).**

The equivalent provision in the *Child Welfare Act* was at s. 52(18).

COMMENTARY:

The Director may delegate authority to another person to do the following:

(a) hold a hearing;
(b) remove the name in, or otherwise amend, the register;
(c) order the society to amend its records, in keeping with the change(s) in (b).

Under the terms of the equivalent provision of the *Child Welfare Act* the delegate could

(a) hold a hearing;
(b) remove the name or amend the register;
(c) specify parties to the hearing;
(d) cause notice of hearing to be given;
(e) order the society to amend its records accordingly.

As can be seen from the above-listed functions, under the old Act the Director's delegate could determine the parties and arrange for notice to be given to the persons specified. Under the new Act, given the reference in s. 72(6) to the application of the *Statutory Powers Procedures Act* R.S.O. 1980, c. 484, these matters must be attended to in connection with any hearing.

S. 72(6): Application of Statutory Powers Procedure Act

(6) *The Statutory Powers Procedure Act* **applies to a hearing and a hearing shall be conducted in accordance with the prescribed practices and procedures.**

The equivalent provision of the *Child Welfare Act* was at s. 52(14).

COMMENTARY:

This subsection simply expresses that the hearing held under s. 72 will be conducted in accordance with the provisions of the *Statutory Powers Procedure Act* R.S.O. 1980, c. 484. The *Child Welfare Act* similarly required adherence to this procedural statute.

S. 72(7): Parties

(7) **The parties to a hearing are,**
    (a) **the registered person;**
    (b) **the society that verified the information referring to or identifying the registered person; and**
    (c) **any other person specified by the Director.**

The equivalent provision in the *Child Welfare Act* was at s. 52(15).

COMMENTARY:

There are no major changes to the list of persons stipulated as parties. A slight change has been adopted in that it is the society that *investigated* the reported abuse that is made a party under s. 72(7). Under s. 52(15) it was the society that *received* the information that was a specified party.

It is of interest that under s. 52(16) of the old Act, notice of a hearing had to be given at least ten days before the hearing date. There is a similar time period in the new Act, in s. 72(4)(b).

S. 72(8): Director's Decision

(8) **Where the Director determines, after holding a hearing, that the information in the register with respect to a registered person is in error or should not be in the register, the Director shall remove the registered person's name from or otherwise amend the register, and may order that the society's records be amended to reflect the Director's decision.**

The equivalent provision in the *Child Welfare Act* was at s. 52(17).

COMMENTARY:

The meaning is the same in both the old and new provisions. After a hearing, the Director (or delegate) may,

(1) determine the information in the register is in error (or presumably that it is not in error);
(2) direct that the name be deleted or otherwise amend the register;
(3) order that the society amend its records accordingly.

It is interesting to observe that s. 72(8) seems to provide an alternative in that the Director may decide that the information is not in error but that the information "should not be in the register." It is not clear what circumstances would give rise to such a decision.

S. 72(9): Appeal to Divisional Court

(9) **A party to a hearing may appeal the Director's decision to the Divisional Court.**

The equivalent provision in the *Child Welfare Act* was at s. 52(19).

COMMENTARY:

This provision is self-explanatory. There is no change from the predecessor legislation.

S. 72(10): Hearing in Private

(10) A hearing or appeal under this section shall be held in the absence of the public and no media representative shall be permitted to attend.

There was no equivalent provision in the *Child Welfare Act.*

COMMENTARY:

This is a new qualification, specifying that a hearing or an appeal from a hearing, of the registration of the name of any registered person who has or may have abused a child, is to be held in private, and no member of the media is permitted to attend.

While the hearing is not a judicial proceeding, it is, at least arguably, *quasi*-judicial in that it is conducted in accordance with the *Statutory Powers Procedure Act* R.S.O. 1980, c. 484. Moreover, an appeal heard by the Divisional Court is certainly a judicial proceeding. Thus, the question arises as to whether this provision will withstand a *Charter of Rights* challenge, based on the freedom of the press rights and privileges.

S. 72(11): Publication

(11) No person shall publish or make public information that has the effect of identifying a witness at or a participant in a hearing, or a party to a hearing other than a society.

There was no equivalent provision in the *Child Welfare Act.*

COMMENTARY:

This provision is a natural consequence of s. 72(10), protecting persons who might otherwise be reluctant to voluntarily report possible abuse if there were a possibility of media exposure.

S. 72(12): Exception to Record Inadmissible

(12) The record of a hearing or appeal under this section shall not be admitted into evidence in any other proceeding except a proceeding under clause 81(1)(d) (confidentiality of register) or clause 81(1)(e) (amendment of society's records).

The equivalent provision under the *Child Welfare Act* was at s. 52(21).

COMMENTARY:

There are no significant changes between this and the *Child Welfare*

Act. The hearing or appeal record is inadmissible in any other proceeding. The only exceptions are:

(1) in a prosecution for failure to comply with s. 71(6) – maintaining confidentiality of register or s. 71(10) – misuse of the register by a person engaged in research; or
(2) in a prosecution for failure to comply with the Director's decision rendered under s. 72(8).

SECTION 73. POWERS OF DIRECTOR

This section gives power to the Director, as defined in s. 3(1)13. of the Act, to transfer a child between societies or between "placements", and cites criteria for such transfers.

S. 73

(1) **A Director may direct, in the best interests of a child in the care or supervision of a society, that the child,**
    (a) **be transferred to the care or supervision of another society; or**
    (b) **be transferred from one placement to another placement designated by the Director.**
(2) **In determining whether to direct a transfer under clause (1)(b), the Director shall take into account,**
    (a) **the length of time the child has spent in the existing placement;**
    (b) **the views of the foster parents; and**
    (c) **the views and preferences of the child, where they are reasonably ascertainable.**

There was no equivalent section under the *Child Welfare Act.*

COMMENTARY:

Under the *Child Welfare Act,* a Director was appointed by the authority of the Minister and had duties as prescribed by statute under s. 2(1). Under the new Act, a Director is defined at s. 3(1) 13. and is appointed by the Minister under s. 5(1). While the statute at Part I does not itemize specific duties as it did under the old legislation, it reserves to the Minister the right to impose "any conditions or limitations" on an appointment, at s. 5(3). It can be expected that duties will be prescribed by regulation.

However, from time to time in different sections of Part III, other specific rights and responsibilities fall to the Director.

The "Director" referred to in ss. 71 and 72 by virtue of the definition at s. 71(1)(a) and s. 71(2), may not be the same person as the "Director" referred to in the other sections of Part III. However, for purposes of all the other sections, including the present s. 73, the Director is as defined in the Act at s. 3.

Section 73 gives the Director power to transfer a child who is in the care or supervision of a society,

(1)   from one society to another;
(2)   from one placement to another.

The Act does not, at either Part I or III, define the term "placement" for the purposes of s. 73(1)(b). Its ordinary meaning would suggest the place where the child resides. Further, the definition of "place of safety" at s. 37(1)(e) and of "residential service" at s. 3(1)25. may provide helpful examples of what is implied in the term "placement".

The criteria to be applied in a transfer of placement are outlined at s. 73(2)(a) through (c). The "best interests of a child" as included in the opening words of s. 73(1) would govern. The importance of foster parent input on transfer already referred to at s. 57(7) again is a factor. A child having some capability to express a view or preference shall also be taken into account at s. 73(2)(c).

It would appear that criteria of s. 73(2), applicable in the first instance to decisions under s. 73(1)(b), must also be applied where the Director exercises his or her authority under s. 57(6).

Since there is a similarity between s. 57(6) and s. 73(1), why is the latter needed? On close inspection, it may be seen that there are distinct differences:

(1)   s. 57(6) is restricted to circumstances of a society "having care of a child", while s. 73(1) is much broader to cover "a child in the care or *supervision* of a society";

Is the wording employed in s. 73(1) broad enough to permit a Director, without any court review or approval, to *remove* a child from a placement and, in so doing, to (in effect) change the child's status from supervision to society wardship? This flies in the face of the purpose of a s. 60 review. It would seem that the word "placement" must be restricted to foster placement, given the conjunctive wording of s. 73(2).

Other differences include:

(2)   the authority in s. 57(6) may be exercised by either a Director or a local director. The authority in s. 73(1) may be used only by a Director.
(3)   There are no criteria beyond "best interests" spelled out in s. 57(6) as there are in s. 73(2). Both used "best interests" as the

starting test. However, having regard for the balance of subsections in s. 57 it may be argued that the criteria in s. 73(2) are adequately considered or available in a placement move authorized by s. 57(6).

If the provisions of s. 73(1) are not for the purpose of permitting the Director to move a child under "supervision" by a parent (and hence preserve the integrity of the review system under s. 60), then much of the section is similar to s. 57(6). If it adds little why is it there, other than to emphasize separately and distinctly, the power of a Director? The section may be used by a Director where there is some conflict between the Ministry and an individual society.

SECTION 74. HOMEMAKERS

This section provides an alternative under which a person entering premises under s. 40, may, instead of taking a child to a place of safety, arrange for a placement of a "homemaker" to care for the child until a protection finding is made.

S. 74

(1)   In this section, "homemaker" means a person who is approved by a Director or local director for the purposes of this section.

(2)   Where it appears to a person entering premises under section 40 that,
    (a)   a child who in the person's opinion is unable to care for himself or herself has been left on the premises without competent care or supervision; and
    (b)   no person having charge of the child is available or able to consent to the placement of a homemaker on the premises,
the person may, instead of taking the child to a place of safety,
    (c)   remain on the premises; or
    (d)   arrange with a society for the placement of a homemaker on the premises.

(3)   A homemaker who remains or is placed on premises under subsection (2) may enter and live there, carry on normal housekeeping activites that are reasonably necessary for the care of any child on the premises and exercise reasonable control and discipline over any such child.

(4)   No action shall be instituted against a homemaker who remains or is placed on premises under subsection (2) for,
    (a)   entering and living on the premises;

(b) anything done or omitted in connection with normal housekeeping activities on the premises;

(c) providing goods and services reasonably necessary for the care of any child on the premises; or

(d) the exercise of reasonable control and discipline over any child on the premises,

so long as the homemaker acts in good faith with reasonable care in the circumstances.

(5) Where a homemaker remains or is placed on premises under subsection (2), the society shall forthwith notify or make reasonable efforts to notify the person last having charge of the child that a homemaker has been placed on the premises.

(6) Where a child with whom a homemaker has been placed under subsection (2),

(a) is found not to be in need of protection, the homemaker shall leave the premises; or

(b) is found to be in need of protection, the court may authorize the homemaker to remain on the premises until,

(i) a specified day not more than thirty days from the date of the order, or

(ii) a person who is entitled to custody of the child returns to care for the child,

whichever is sooner.

(7) Where no person returns to care for the child before the day specified in an order under clause (6)(b), the court may,

(a) extend the order; or

(b) hold a further hearing under section 43 and make an order under section 53.

The equivalent provision of the *Child Welfare Act* was at s. 23.

COMMENTARY:

The old and new laws are comparable but for minor word modification, in every respect. A homemaker's function is to replace a person having charge of a child, who is unable or unavailable to care for a child in the home. The section details these responsibilities:

(1) the circumstances under which the homemaker may remain or be placed; (s. 74(2));

(2) the scope of a homemaker's authority; (s. 74(3));

(3) protection of the homemaker from personal liability; (s. 74(4));

(4) obligation to notify parent upon homemaker placement; (s. 74(5));

(5) court authority to remove or approve homemaker's remaining on premises, depending on protection finding; (s. 74(6));

(6) time-limit for homemaker remaining on premises where protection needed; (s. 74(6)).

Where, on an application under s. 43, the court,

(1) makes a protection finding, it may authorize the homemaker's continued placement for a specified period (s. 74(6)(b));
(2) finds that the child is not in need of protection, the court shall direct that the homemaker leave (s. 74(6)(a)).

SECTION 75. OFFENCES, RESTRAINING ORDERS, RECOVERY ON CHILD'S BEHALF

This section sets down various actions which constitute offences under the Act. These are closely related to "need for protection", though they are not here defined in terms of protection.

S. 75: Offences

s. 75 (1) In this section, "abuse" means a state or condition of being physically harmed, sexually molested or sexually exploited.

(2) No person having charge of a child shall,
   (a) inflict abuse on the child; or
   (b) by failing to care and provide for or supervise and protect the child adequately,
      (i) permit the child to suffer abuse, or
      (ii) permit the child to suffer from a mental, emotional or developmental condition that, if not remedied, could seriously impair the child's development.

(3) No person having charge of a child less than sixteen years of age shall leave the child without making provision for his or her supervision and care that is reasonable in the circumstances.

(4) Where a person is charged with contravening subsection (3) and the child is less than ten years of age, the onus of establishing that the person made provision for the child's supervision and care that was reasonable in the circumstances rests with the person.

(5) No person having charge of a child less than sixteen years of age shall permit the child to,
   (a) loiter in a public place; or
   (b) be in a place of public entertainment, unless accompanied by the person or by an individual eighteen years of age or older who is appointed by the person,
   between the hours of midnight and 6 a.m.

(6) Where a child who is actually or apparently less than

> **sixteen years of age is in a place to which the public has access, unaccompanied by a responsible adult, between the hours of midnight and 6 a.m., a peace officer may apprehend the child without a warrant and proceed as if the child had been apprehended under subsection 40(10) (child under twelve).**
>
> **(7) The court may, in connection with a case arising under subsection (2), (3) or (5), proceed under this Part as if an application had been made under subsection 40(1) (child protection proceeding) in respect of the child.**

This section incorporates the provisions of a number of sections from the *Child Welfare Act,* notably ss. 47, 48 and 54.

COMMENTARY:

This section, in effect, selects certain of the situations originally described in s. 37(2) as indicating a need for protection, and classifies these as offences in their own right, for which penalties are provided. The extent of the penalties is set out in s. 81(1)(f) and (2).

   The method of doing this is similar to what had been used in the *Child Welfare Act* at s. 47(1). The word "abuse" is once again defined, this time for purposes of s. 75 only. The definition is more restricted than that in s. 68(1) where the purpose is to establish a duty to report such a condition. Section 68(1) defines the term "to suffer abuse", by equating that term with "to be in need of protection", wherever such need arises from any one of five selected clauses of s. 37(2). In s. 75, no reference is made to the "need for protection" or to s. 37(2).

   In essence, the difference between the two definitions of "abuse" is as follows:

Section 68(1)	*Section 75(1)*
"to suffer abuse" means "to be in need of protection", provided such need arises from any of the following clauses of s. 37(2):	"abuse" means a state or condition of any of the following, without specific reference to protection or to s. 37:
(a) physical harm	(i) physical harm
(c) sexual molestation or exploitation	(ii) sexual molestation or exploitation
(e) need for medical treatment	
(f) emotional harm	
(h) an emotional condition that could impair development.	

Thus, the definition is somewhat narrower where the purpose is to define an offence than where it refers only to a duty to report. The situations involving medical treatment, emotional harm and the child's emotional condition, which would constitute a need for protection and a duty to report, do not constitute the basis for an offence. The penalty provision is at s. 81(2).

In addition to the offences of inflicting, or permitting the inflicting of abuse (s. 75(2)(a), (b)(i)), the permitting of a child "to suffer from a mental, emotional or developmental condition that, if not remedied, could seriously impair the child's development" also constitutes an offence. The wording of the subclause is substantially the same as that found in s. 37(2)(h). Presumably, if a child is found to be in "need of protection" within s. 37(2)(h), then any person permitting such a situation to exist could be guilty of the offence set out in s. 75(2)(b)(ii).

Section 75(3) prohibits the leaving of a child less than 16 years by the person having charge, without adequate provision for supervision and care. This is akin to a need for "protection" as described at s. 37(2)(i). Its provisions are refined at s. 75(4) where, for a child under ten years, the onus to prove that the provision made for the supervision and care of the child was reasonable, rests with the person charged. The penalty for contravention is found at s. 81(1)(f). Hence this is a reverse onus circumstance. The counterpart provisions under the *Child Welfare Act* were at s. 48.

Section 75(5) describes other circumstances, which if occurring, will be subject to penalty under s. 81(1)(f). These circumstances are a carry over from the *Child Welfare Act*, with minor variations:

(1)   s. 75(5)(a) child loitering in public place between midnight and 6 a.m. (see s. 54(2) *Child Welfare Act*);
(2)   s. 75(5)(b): child in a place of public entertainment during the same hours, without an adult (see s. 54(2), *Child Welfare Act*).

The use of "unaccompanied by a responsible adult" in s. 75(6), appears to be addressing the circumstances of the child prostitute out on the streets with his or her pimp (business agent), between certain hours. However, under this Act, circumstances resulting in the child being "apprehended without a warrant" do not, (insofar as the "adult" with whom the child *might* be, is concerned), constitute an offence committed by that adult.

Given s. 75(7) proceedings under this section will be commenced in the same way as child protection proceeding would follow an application under s. 40.

SECTION 76. RESTRAINING ORDERS

This section empowers a court which has found that a "need for protection" exists, to issue an order restricting a person's access to the child. This order may be "instead of or in addition to" an order under s. 53(1). Some special limitations on such orders are set out.

S. 76

(1)   Where the court finds that a child is in need of protection, the court may, instead of or in addition to making an order under subsection 53(1), make an order in the child's best interests restraining or prohibiting a person's access to or contact with the child, and may include in the order such directions as the court considers appropriate for implementing the order and protecting the child.

(2)   An order shall not be made under subsection (1) unless notice of the proceeding has been served personally on the person to be named in the order.

(3)   An order made under subsection (1) shall be in force for a specified period not exceeding six months.

(4)   An application for the extension, variation or termination of an order made under subsection (1) may be made by,

    (a)   the person who is the subject of the order;

    (b)   the child;

    (c)   the person having charge of the child;

    (d)   a society;

    (e)   a Director; or

    (f)   where the child is an Indian or a native person, a representative chosen by the child's band or native community.

(5)   Where an application is made under subsection (4), the court may, in the child's best interests,

    (a)   extend the order for a further period or periods of six months; or

    (b)   vary or terminate the order.

(6)   Where a society has care of a child and an order made under subsection (1) prohibiting a person's access to the child is in force, the society shall not return the child to the care of,

    (a)   the person named in the order; or

    (b)   a person who may permit that person to have access to the child.

There was no equivalent section in the *Child Welfare Act*.

COMMENTARY:

This section supplements the alternatives available to a court when need for protection has been found, by adding to the four orders listed at s. 53(1), a further option – restricted access or contact. In fact, the court's power to make an order restricting access to the child has already been established in s. 54, and the current s. 76 seems largely meant to emphasize that this is an available option "instead of or in addition to" an order under s. 53(1). Otherwise stated, the court has the additional option, whenever a need for protection has been found to exist, to make such a restraining order with or without an order under s. 53(1). Orders made under s. 76(1) have some special limitations.

Firstly, a court may not use this section for any interim proceeding, *i.e.* prior to the protection finding being determined. This has a particularly restrictive effect, most importantly in cases where serious abuse is alleged. The omission of such authority is a serious legislative oversight. A court is obliged to rely upon the provisions of s. 47(5) (see prior discussion) or s. 54(1)(a) and seek a "no-access" order.

Secondly, procedures under s. 76(2) and (3) govern the making of such orders, requiring notice to the person to be named, and providing a maximum term for the order, of six months. An order, upon a review by a court, may be extended for further six-month periods under s. 76(5). Parties entitled to seek a variation, extension or termination of such an order are specified under s. 76(4), and include the person who is the subject of the order.

A society is prohibited under s. 76(6), from placing a child in its care with a person whose access is restrained under s. 76(1).

As in s. 54, any order restraining access, under s. 76(1), must be made "in the child's best interests."

Given the wording of s. 76(1) such order would normally be considered and made (if applied) at a protection hearing's disposition stage. The implication is that it is a remedy not available in a review as under s. 60. How broadly a court will interpret s. 76(1) will determine whether such is the case or not.

SECTION 77. RECOVERY ON CHILD'S BEHALF FOR ABUSE

This section provides the avenue for legal action on a child's behalf where the child has suffered abuse. The latter is defined in terms of five of the conditions which constitute need for protection at s. 37(2).

S. 77

(1)   In this section, "to suffer abuse", when used in reference to a child, means to be in need of protection within the meaning of clause 37(2)(a), (c), (e), (f) or (h).

(2) When the Official Guardian is of the opinion that a child has a cause of action or other claim because the child has suffered abuse, the Official Guardian may, if he or she considers it to be in the child's best interests, institute and conduct proceedings on the child's behalf for the recovery of damages or other componention.

(3) Where a child is in a society's care and custody, subsection (2) also applies to the society with necessary modifications.

The equivalent provision in the *Child Welfare Act* was at s. 51.

COMMENTARY:

In the new Act the "abuse" upon which an action on behalf of a child is based, goes back to the meaning of protection at s. 37(2)(a), (c), (e), (f) or (h). In short, circumstances of:

(1) physical harm;
(2) sexual molestation or exploitation;
(3) absence or refusal to obtain medical treatment;
(4) emotional harm; or
(5) unavailability or refusal to obtain treatment for a mental, emotional or developmental condition;

experienced by a child, shall constitute the abuse. The definition of "to suffer abuse" in this section is identical to that used in s. 68(1). It is much broader than the "abuse" as defined under s. 47(1) of the *Child Welfare Act* upon which s. 51 of that Act was based.

In the new Act, the applicant on behalf of an abused child will be either:

(1) the Official Guardian; or
(2) a society, where the child is in its care and custody.

The Official Guardian has jurisdiction in any case. The rights of a society are limited to cases where a child is a society or Crown ward. The test to be applied to the decision to institute and conduct proceedings is two-fold:

(1) has abuse occurred?
(2) is the commencement of proceedings in "the child's best interests"?

In applying the "best interests" criterion, reference must be had to the provisions of s. 37(3). The relief to be sought will be damages or "other compensation."

What are the child's rights where either the Official Guardian or a society (in whose care the child is), fails to exercise rights under this section to sue for damages on the child's behalf? Is a society ever obliged to commence a proceeding where the child has suffered or sustained *some* damage, but the extent and degree of the injury or the duration of wardship are minimal? Will the society be obliged to provide counsel and financing for the child's lawsuit? Is this section without limits and guidelines?

SECTION 78. PROHIBITION ON PLACEMENT

This section provides that a child cannot be placed in a society's care and custody except as provided in this Act.

S. 78

No person shall place a child in the care and custody of a society, and no society shall take a child into its care and custody, except,
(a)   in accordance with this Part; or
(b)   under an agreement made under subsection 29(1) or 30(1) (temporary care or special needs agreement) of Part II (Voluntary Access to Services).

The equivalent provision of the *Child Welfare Act* was at s. 26.

COMMENTARY:

In the new Act a child may not be taken into the care and custody of a society unless as specifically prescribed under s. 78. Its predecessor was of the same effect.

In addition, the provisions of s. 78(b) sanction placement where the agreements specified apply. These are agreements under Part II of the Act for voluntary services to a child or family.

SECTION 79. OFFENCES RELATED TO INTERFERENCE WITH A CHILD

This section forbids any attempt to thwart an order for supervision or wardship through contact or interference with the child.

S. 79

Where a child is the subject of an order for society supervision, society wardship or Crown wardship under subsection 53(1), no person shall,
(a)   induce or attempt to induce the child to leave the care of the

person with whom the child is placed by the court or by the society as the case may be;

(b)   detain or harbour the child after the person or society referred to in clause (a) requires that the child be returned;

(c)   interfere with the child or remove or attempt to remove the child from any place; or

(d)   for the purpose of interfering with the child, visit or communicate with the person referred to in clause (a).

The equivalent provision in the *Child Welfare Act* was at s. 46.

COMMENTARY:

The critical difference between this section and its counterpart s. 46 of the *Child Welfare Act* is that the prohibitions (a) through (d) of s. 79 are absolute. The proviso at the end of s. 46 permitted the actions (a) through (d) if a society consented in writing. A society or person seeking to circumvent the proscriptions of s. 79 must seek a court amendment of the order under s. 53(1) to which s. 79 applies.

The word "interfere" in s. 79(c) can be given a broad meaning and may include acts by any person, including written or oral communications by telephone, with the child.

However, the limitation in the new section as against the old is the required ingredient that an order under subsection 53(1) must be in place before the section becomes operative. Section 46 of the old Act had no such limitation, but applied only to circumstances where the society had "the care, custody or supervision of the child." The new section thus offers no sanction for such interference during the course of proceedings, (including interim or temporary placement proceedings) prior to the court order being made under s. 53(1).

SECTION 80. OTHER OFFENCES

S. 80

No person shall,

(a)   knowingly give false information in an application under this Part; or

(b)   obstruct, interfere with or attempt to obstruct or interfere with a child protection worker who is acting under section 40.

The *Child Welfare Act* counterpart was s. 94(1)(a) and (d).

COMMENTARY:

The provisions of the new Act must be read concomitantly with s. 81(1)(i), where the penalties are applied for such offences. There is no substantive difference between old and new Acts.

SECTION 81. PENALTIES FOR OFFENCES

S. 81

(1)   A person who contravenes,
(a)   an order for access made under subsection 54(1);
(b)   subsection 68(3) (reporting child abuse);
(c)   subsection 70(5) (disclosure of information obtained by court order);
(d)   subsection 71(6) or (10) (confidentiality of child abuse register);
(e)   an order made under subsection 72(8) (amendment of society's records);
(f)   subsection 75(3) or (5) (leaving child unattended, etc.);
(g)   a restraining order made under subsection 76(1);
(h)   section 78 (unauthorized placement);
(i)   any provision of section 79 (interference with child, etc.); or
(j)   clause 80(a) or (b),
and a director, officer or employee of a corporation who authorizes, permits or concurs in such a contravention by the corporation is guilty of an offence and on conviction is liable to a fine of not more than $1,000 or, except in the case of a contravention of subsection 68(3), to imprisonment for a term of not more than one year, or to both.

(2)   A person who contravenes subsection 75(2) (child abuse), and a director, officer or employee of a corporation who authorizes, permits or concurs in such a contravention by the corporation is guilty of an offence and on conviction is liable to a fine of not more than $2,000 or to imprisonment for a term of not more than two years, or to both.

(3)   A person who contravenes subsection 41(8) or 72(11) (publication of identifying information) or an order prohibiting publication made under clause 41(7)(c) or subsection 41(9), and a director, officer or employee of a corporation who authorizes, permits or concurs in such a contravention by the corporation, is guilty of an offence and on conviction is liable to a fine of not more than $10,000 or to imprisonment for a term of not more than three years, or to both.

The equivalent provision in the *Child Welfare Act* was found in parts of s. 94.

S. 81(1): Penalty Provisions: Lesser Offences

Under the new Act, persons found guilty of an offence under subsection 81(1) may be fined up to $1,000. The offence of failing to report child abuse is subject to the same monetary penalty, or imprisonment for a term of one year, or both. These same penalties were imposed by s. 94(1) of the *Child Welfare Act* for its counterpart offences.

S. 81(2) and (3): Penalty Provisions: More Serious Offences

Offences under subsections (2) and (3) are considered more serious and call for higher penalties. Subsection (2) refers to child abuse under subsection 75(2) (penalty: fine up to $2,000, or two years in prison, or both). Subsection (3) refers to prohibited publication of information, dealt with in four separate subsections of the Act, (penalty: fine up to $10,000 or three years in prison, or both). Both the above apply as well to a director, officer or employee of a corporation.

SECTION 82. CHILD'S RELIGIOUS FAITH

This section stipulates the guidelines for the determination of a child's religion. In addition, it prohibits placement of children of a particular religious background into conflicting foster homes.

S. 82

(1) For the purposes of this section, a child shall be deemed to have the religious faith agreed upon by the child's parent, but where there is no agreement or the court cannot readily determine what the religious faith agreed upon is or whether any religious faith is agreed upon, the court may decide what the child's religious faith is, if any, on the basis of the child's circumstances.

(2) The court shall consider the child's views and wishes, if they can be reasonably ascertained, in determining what the child's religious faith is, if any.

(3) A Protestant child shall not be committed under this Part to the care of a Roman Catholic society or institution and a Roman Catholic child shall not be committed under this Part to a Protestant society or institution, and a Protestant child shall not be placed in a foster home with a Roman Catholic family and a Roman Catholic child shall not be placed in a foster home with a Protestant family, and, where a child committed under this Part is other than Protestant or Roman

Catholic, the child shall be placed where practicable with a family of his or her own religious faith, if any.

(4) Subsection (3) does not apply to the commitment of a child to the care of a society in a municipality in which there is only one society.

(5) Where a society,

(a) is unable to place a child in a suitable foster home within a reasonable time because of the operation of subsection (3); and

(b) would be able to place the child in a suitable foster home but for the operation of subsection (3),

the society may apply to a Director who may order that subsection (3) does not apply to the child in respect of the placement.

The *Child Welfare Act* equivalent was s. 44.

COMMENTARY:

1. *Determination of Child's Religious Faith:* The new law has effected important changes to this determination. Under the *Child Welfare Act*, s. 44(1) and (2), the determination followed these principles:

(1) For a child born of persons married to one another the child's faith was *deemed* to be that of the father; (see s. 44(1));

(2) the exceptions to (1) applied where there was a written agreement between the parents that the child's faith was to be that of the mother; (see s. 44(1));

(3) For a child born outside of a marriage the child's faith was *deemed* to be that of the mother; (see s. 44(2));

(4) A court might disregard the provisions of s. 44(1) and (2) where it found on the child's wishes that some other determination ought to be made (see s. 44(7)).

Under the *Child and Family Services Act*, the route is streamlined:

(1) A child's religious faith is *deemed* to be that as the child's parents have agreed upon (see s. 82(1)); or

(2) Where,

(a) there is no agreement; or

(b) a court can't readily determine what the faith agreed upon is, or whether any agreement is in existence;

the court may arrive at its own determination taking into account the child's circumstances (see s. 82(1));

(3) The court is obliged to consider the "views and wishes" of the child in its determination.

The antiquated "deeming" provisions of the old Act, based on a parent's sex are gone (see s. 82(2) of the new Act). Agreement of the parents or the child's circumstances and wishes, become the basis of any determination.

2. *Placement:* The rules as to placement found in s. 82(3), (4) and (5), with but minor modification, are identical to their *Child Welfare Act* counterparts in s. 44(4), (5) and (6).

Section 82(5) is new to the extent that it no longer falls upon the court to make such exception orders. These may be dealt with by a Director.

SECTION 83. INJUNCTIONS

This section provides the Supreme Court authority for injunctive relief.

S. 83

(1) The Supreme Court may grant an injunction to restrain a person from contravening section 79, on the society's application.
(2) The Supreme Court may vary or terminate an order made under subsection (1), on any person's application.

The *Child Welfare Act* equivalent was s. 95(1).

COMMENTARY:

The old and new address essentially a prohibition on similar conduct (see discussion s. 79 Offence: to interfere with a child under supervision or in care of a society; *Child Welfare Act* counterpart s. 46).

The jurisdiction for injunctive relief is vested exclusively in the Supreme Court. Any order made may be varied.

TABLE OF CONCORDANCE

C.F.S.A.	C.W.A.	C.F.S.A.	C.W.A.
s. 37(1)(a)	s. 19(1)(a)	38(5)	19(4)
s. 37(1)(b)	s. 1(1)(f)	39(1)	28(3)
s. 37(1)(c)		39(2)	
s. 37(1)(d)	s. 19(1)(e)	39(3)	28(3)(6)(8), 35(1)(6), 37(1)(5), 38(2)(6)
s. 37(1)(e)	s. 19(1)(f)(g)	39(4)	28(7), 33, 35(5), 37(4), 38(4)
s. 37(2)(a)	s. 19(1)(b)		
s. 37(2)(b)		39(5)	28(7), 33
s. 37(2)(c)	s. 19(1)(b)(iv)(v)(xi)	39(6)	
s. 37(2)(d)		39(7)	28(10)(16), 37(3)
s. 37(2)(e)	s. 19(1)(b)(ix)	40(1)	
s.37(2)(f)	s. 19(1)(b)(x)	40(2)	22(1)
s. 37(2)(g)		40(3)	22(2)
s. 37(2)(h)		40(4)	22(4)
s. 37(2)(i)	s. 19(1)(b)(ii)(iii)	40(5)	22(3)
s. 37(2)(j)		40(6)	21(1)(a), (2)
s. 37(2)(k)		40(7)	
s. 37(2)(1)	s. 19(1)(b)(i)	40(8)	
s. 37(3) :1	s. 1(1)(b)(i)	40(9)	
s. 37(3) :2	s. 1(1)(b)(iii)	40(10)	
s. 37(3) :3		40(11)	
s. 37(3) :4		40(12)	
s. 37(3) :5	s. 1(1)(b)(vii)	40(13)	ss. 21(2), 22(1)(b)
s. 37(3) :6		40(14)	ss. 21(3), 22(3)
s. 37(3) :7	s. 1(1)(b)(iv)	40(15)	
s. 37(3) :8	1(1)(b)(v)	40(16)	
s. 37(3) :9	1(1)(b)(vi)	40(17)	s. 21(1)
s. 37(3) :10	1(1)(b)(vii)		
s. 37(3) :11	1(1)(b)(viii)	41(1)	s. 57(4)(5)
s. 37(3) :12		41(2)	
s. 37(3) :13		41(3)	s. 57(1)
s. 37(3)		41(4)	s. 57(2)
s. 38(1)	20(1)	41(5)	s. 57(4)
s. 38(2)	20(2)	41(6)	s. 57(5)
s. 38(3)		41(7)	
s. 38(4)	20(3)	41(8)	s. 57(7)

C.F.S.A.	C.W.A.	C.F.S.A.	C.W.A.
s. 41(9)	s. 57(7)(b)	54(7)	
s. 41(10)			
s. 42(1)	s. 27(1)	55(1)	
s. 42(2)	s. 27(2)	55(2)	
s. 43(1)	s. 28(1)	56(1)	s. 31(1)
s. 43(2)	s. 28(1)	56(2)	s. 31(2)
s. 43(3)			
s. 44(1)			
s. 44(2)	19(2)	56(3)	s. 31(3)
s. 44(3)	19(3)		
s. 44(4)	30(1) :1, 2	56(4)	s. 31(4)
s. 45	28(2)	56(5)	s. 31(5)
s. 46(1)	28(4)	56(6)	s. 31(6)
s. 46(2)		57(1)	
s. 47(1)	28(13)	57(2)	40(1)
s. 47(2)	28(12)	57(3)	45(1)
s. 47(3)		57(4)	45(2), 40(2)
s. 47(4)		57(5)	
s. 47(5)	28(12)	57(6)	45(2)
s. 47(6)	28(14)	57(7)	
s. 47(7)	28(15)	57(8)	
s. 48		57(9)	
s. 49(1)	30(4)(5), 36	57(10)	
s. 49(2)		58(1)	
s. 50(1)	29(1)	58(2)	
s. 50(2)	29(1)	58(3)	
s. 50(3)	29(2)	58(4)	
s. 50(4)	29(3)	59(1)	40(1)
s. 50(5)	29(3)	59(2)	41
s. 50(6)	29(4)	60(1)	
s. 50(7)	29(5)	60(2)	32(1)(2), 37(1), 38(2)
s. 50(8)	29(4)		
s. 51	s. 30(5)	60(3)	32(3)
s. 52	s. 30(5)	60(4)	32(4), 37(2), 38(1)
s. 53(1)	s. 30(1)	60(5)	
s. 53(2)	s. 30(5)	60(6)	32(1)(5)(7), 37(1)(2)(4)(5), 38(1)(2)(3)(4)(6)
s. 53(3)			
s. 53(4)			
s. 53(5)		60(7)(8)	32(4), 37(2), 38(1)(2)
s. 53(6)			
s. 53(7)		60(9)	
s. 53(8)	s. 30(4)	60(10)	37(6)(9)
s. 53(9)		61(1)(2)	s. 32(1), 37(1), 38(2)
s. 54(1)	s. 35(1)(4)	61(3)	s. 32(1), 37(1), 35(1)
s. 54(2)	s. 35(1)	62(1)(2)	s. 39
s. 54(3)	s. 35(1)	63(1)	s. 3(1)
s. 54(4)	s. 35(5)(6)	63(2)	s. 3(2)
s. 54(5)	s. 35(2)	64(1)	
s. 54(6)	s. 35(3)	64(2)	

C.F.S.A.	C.W.A.	C.F.S.A.	C.W.A.
s. 64(3)		72(2)	s. 52(12)
s. 65(1)	s. 43(1)	72(3)	s. 52(13)
s. 65(2)		72(4)	s. 52(14)
s. 65(3)	s. 43(2)(3)	72(5)	s. 52(15)
s. 65(4)	s. 43(4)	72(6)	s. 52(16)
s. 65(5)		72(7)	s. 52(17)
s. 65(6)	s. 43(8)	72(8)	s. 52(18)
s. 65(7)	s. 43(1)	72(9)	s. 52(19)
s. 65(8)		72(10)	
s. 66(1)	s. 30(1) :2	72(11)	
s. 66(2)	s. 30(2), 37(1)	72(12)	s. 52(21)
s. 66(3)	s. 43(5), 37(3)	73(1)	
s. 67(1)(2)	s. 42	73(2)	
s. 68(1)		74(1)	s. 23(1)
s. 68(2)	s. 49(1)	74(2)	s. 23(2)
s. 68(3)	s. 49(2)	74(3)	s. 23(3)
s. 68(4)		74(4)	s. 23(5)
s. 68(5)		74(5)	s. 23(6)
s. 68(6)		74(6)	s. 23(7)
s. 68(7)	s. 49(3)	74(7)	s. 23(8)
s. 68(8)	s. 49(4)	75(1)	s. 47(1)
s. 69(1)		75(2)	s. 47(2)
s. 69(2)		75(3)	s. 48(1)
s. 69(3)		75(4)	s. 48(3)
s. 69(4)		75(5)	54(2)
s. 69(5)		75(6)	54(1)
s. 69(6)		75(7)	47(3), 48(2), 54(3)
s. 69(7)		76(1)	
s. 70(1)		76(2)	
s. 70(2)		76(3)	
s. 70(3)	50(1)	76(4)	
s. 70(4)		76(5)	
s. 70(5)	50(3)(2)	76(6)	
s. 70(6)		77(1)	51
s. 70(7)	50(4)	77(2)	51
s. 71(1)	52(1)	77(3)	51
s. 71(2)		78	26
s. 71(3)	52(2)	79	46
s. 71(4)	52(2)	80	94(1)(a)(d)
s. 71(5)	52(3)	81(1)	94(1)
s. 71(6)	52(4)	81(2)	94(2)
s. 71(7)	52(5)	81(3)	94(6)
s. 71(8)	52(6)	82(1)	44(1)(3)
s. 71(9)		82(2)	44
s. 71(10)	52(7)	82(3)	44(4)
s. 71(11)	52(8)	82(4)	44(5)
s. 71(12)	52(9)	82(5)	
s. 71(13)	52(10)	83(1)(2)	95(1)
s. 71(14)	52(11)		
s. 72(1)			

INDEX

FAMILY
see also Extended Family
not defined in Act, 6

FOSTER HOME
place of safety, 9
removal of child from – notice,
105, 107

FOSTER PARENT
party to Part III proceeding, 30
right to review prior to child's
removal, 105, 107
views required before placement
transfer, 152
wishes to be taken into account
where child is Crown ward, 105,
107-108

HEARING
see also Evidence, Media, Notice,
Parties
adjournment of, 67-76
assessments during, 79-84
delay exceeding three months, 77
evidence at, 64-67
information required in protection
hearing, 57-60
place of – territorial jurisdiction, 61
private, unless otherwise ordered,
51-53
separation from hearings in
criminal proceedings, 50
transcripts restricted, 54
transfer between jurisdictions, 62

HOMEMAKER
definition and function, 154-156
time limit to remain on premises,
55

INDIAN OR NATIVE CHILDREN
best interests criteria, 26
restriction on placement, 93-94
status review application, 114, 116

JURISDICTION
affecting court orders of placement,
62
meaning of, 60
related to place of hearing, 61
status review applications, 114

LEGAL REPRESENTATION
child's right to, 26-30
entitlement of child to participate
at hearing, 35

MEDIA
choosing representative to be
present at hearing, 51-53
defined, 50
exclusion from hearing by order,
51-53
restriction on identifying persons
charged, 54

MEDICAL TREATMENT
need of, as circumstance of
protection, 12

NOTICE
also see Hearing
child 12 or over, 33
child under 12, 34
dispensing with, 35
right to receive, for proceedings
under Part III, 30-36
wardship orders restricted where
notice dispensed with, 95-96

OFFENCES
general, 156-158, 163-164
penalties for offences, 164-165

OPEN TEMPORARY DETENTION,
PLACE OF
see Place of Safety

ORDER
expiry of, at age 18 or marriage,
130-131
optional orders where child in
need of protection, 89-97
principal orders under *Child and
Family Services Act* (Part III)
listed, 4
removal order restricted on
protection finding, 92

PARENT
also see Foster Parent
definition, 6-8
restricted, 116
status review application, 114

175